Planting a Multicultural Church

Planting a Multicultural Church

A practical guide to planting a multicultural church in today's modern world. This books covers the need of the United Pentecostal Church to be at the forefront of reaching the world in our own backyard.

Dan Scott

Planting a Multicultural Church

© 2006, Home Missions Division

All Scripture quotations in this book are from the King James Version of the Bible unless otherwise noted.

All rights reserved. No portion of this publication may be reproduced, stored in an electronic system, or transmitted in any form or by any means, electronic, mechanical, photocopy, recording, or otherwise, without the prior permission of the Home Missions Division. Brief quotations may be used in literary reviews.

Printed in the United States of America

ISBN #: 0757722571

Table of Contents

Introduction, Multicultural Church Planting 7

What Is Multicultural Ministries 11

Whose World Are We Evangelizing? 17

The Church's Purpose 25

Immigrants, Or Future In The Making 31

New Dimensions In World Evangelism 43

International is a Big Word 53

Strategies That Serve Our Best Interests 57

Calculated Changes 65

Surrendering Our Prejudice 71

The Church is a Global Community 77

Evangelism Into The Black Community 87

The Asian Revival 95

Evangelism to the North American Native Indian Culture 101

A History of Some Emerging Ministries 111

The Need Of A Cultural Bridge 115

Evangelism, Revival, And Multicultural Ministries 121

The Jesus Method 131

Some Strategy For Multicultural Church Planting 135

The Plan 143

Sharing Facilities With A Daughter Church 151

INTRODUCTION
Multicultural Church Planting

Upon the battlefront in which we find ourselves as pastors, there are violent struggles as we expend our resources to reach the whole world with the whole gospel. At times, there are counter-positions to take that defy the very balance of self-esteem. We know our failures too well to boast of the past; and our victories, while many, have been too few to give permanent feelings of security.

Among the many issues that confront us, we as United Pentecostals must address the all-important subject of the variegated society that has forced a changing face upon North America. The field of evangelism as a result of these changes has taken on different proportions.

The challenge now facing the church in the spiritual arena is to achieve a blending of these different nationalities and cultures into the local church body. Many of these will ultimately result in autonomous churches for specific cultures— that being inevitable— but we can participate as never before in establishing a program that will multiply harvest results with distinct advantage in language and custom expertise. This is our job, and when the task has been accomplished the local churches will emerge with the benefits; they will shepherd some of the greatest congregations ever dreamed possible!

Within the Black community there is a feeling that the United Pentecostal Church is the answer to the promise of the aged Apostle Paul, a church "...where there is neither Jew nor Greek, bond or free..." The future looms beautifully as the body of Christ emerges as a spiritual family, embracing the people of all cultures without exclusion. We, as a church, must dedicate ourselves to create that kind of atmosphere from every sector.

The Spanish language, the third largest language group in the world, has now established in North America a Spanish speaking nation much larger than the majority of those countries our missionaries are commissioned to evangelize. In this we are standing somewhere sandwiched between the opportunities it represents and the responsibilities it will exact from us.

Dealing with the problems of assimilating the results of Multicultural Ministries into the fellowship, we have made important inroads. We are now dealing with second-generation Spanish constituents who know no other church home, and that has been the product of an established direction. The Filipino living in the United States and Canada are under a solid leadership and blend well with the domestic church. In the Asian communities we are merely touching the tip of the iceberg due the fact that most of this culture has little, if any, knowledge of the Christian heritage. However, now that we are aware of this, it will arm us with the patience necessary to reap a bountiful harvest. We are slowly making progress in French evangelism, and it is expected to have a continual growth. The Native American Indian Ministries while making strides must cover a lot of ground to take its place in the body as the Lord would have it. And, the list goes on.

We are building a strong variegated-cultural body within the fellowship, and for this, the United Pentecostal Church will rise to give the General Home Mission Division and its leadership a vote of gratitude. However, while we are enjoying a productive cross-cultural ministry, we have not yet attained the goals so necessary to a permanent success.

We spend countless thousands on the mission of the church to a world outside the walls of our culture (and rightly so), but there is a glance I would have you to take from the back doors of your church. There is a miniature world out there made up of those same peoples. This world is melting into an already established internal people composite known as the Ten Nations of North America: (1) Quebec (2) New England (3) Appalachia (4 Dixie (5) Black America (6) Steel Belt (7) Corn Belt (8) Northwest (9) Mexican American /Latin/Caribbean (10) Asian/Pacific Rim. With a little understanding and cultural tolerance we can evangelize this populace, and place ready-made missionaries in virtually every corner of the world from the results, as well as have a church in North America that reflects the church of Revelations 7.

I am thankful for the church's vision in these important days just prior to the coming of the Lord. It is demonstrating burden and urgency for the spiritual needs of those of our multicultural populations, as well as a genuine love void of prejudice.

Chapter One
What Is Multicultural Ministries

Cross-culture evangelism, or what we call Multicultural Ministries, is a dream whose time has come! For far too long we have ignored this one great evangelism program that has the capability to perform the task of evangelizing the world.

If we are to complete the responsibility the risen Lord entrusted to the church, we must realize that the ability to perform the command is beyond the vernacular. Even from biblical days, Christ instituted a ministry that involved the evangelized. He stunned the world by merely sending them "home" to tell their house what great things the Lord had done in their lives. A demoniac incapable of self-determination relating to his future.... a woman at a well on a merry-go-round of instability.... and a fisherman hungry to see his world touched by the promised Messiah. Each went in search of family and friends to "tell them" they had come in contact with "a man". The results became important segments of the church's history!

Cross-culture evangelism is a daring dream anxious to be exposed, as well as an awesome undertaking requiring a tremendous spirit of unity on the part of the church. The success of this mission depends upon every person in the United Pentecostal Church International becoming committed to the purpose. It is a program that is both bold and exciting, yet realistic and attainable.

Cross-culture evangelism is biblical, and fulfills the great commission. Its pattern was first established in Christ's earthly ministry, and then later duplicated by the principle advocates of the Book of Acts. Moreover, the results of cross-culture evangelism will provide our Foreign Missions Division with personnel far more productive than even the 'trained' missionaries who spend years dedicated to a task others were born to perform.

The increasingly diverse multicultural population of our major cities can be turned around within the circles of the United Pentecostal Church International to become the solution rather than the problem. It is indeed a daring dream whose time has come!

I became involved in this special ministry in 1979. My activity during that early period was received with much heartache and distrust. I was told my views were absolutely too bold to be implemented with confidence by the constituency, that the vision I embraced needed time to be drawn into a concept. Yet in 1986, The General Home Missions Division and The Western District of the UPCI were impacted to the possibilities, and became innovative co-sponsors of this attainable goal. The Western District Board, chaired by a farsighted superintendent, gave credibility and emphasis to this ministry on a local scale, and accepted the challenge to patiently work out the details. The pilot program was modified several times until the inroads were clearly defined in order that others could follow. This pilot program of cross-cultural evangelism was called Special Ministries.

And, follow, North America did! Cross-culture evangelism is now perhaps one of the most talked about programs in the UPCI! Many are now feeling what the Western District felt in 1986. A massive revival can indeed be given birth and transported worldwide by our multicultural population! Now that it has gained the momentum of calculated successes, we must continue to be the innovative leader by providing our constituency with an example of leadership in this endeavor.

Multicultural Ministries (known at that time as Special Ministries) became an evangelistic arm of the Western District. Working under the canopy of the district Home Missions Department, one of its mandates was to serve faithfully and effectively to evangelize the various cultures living within the district boundaries. No desire was incorporated to change administrational policies embraced by the present system. The program was based upon coordination for evangelism, and would divorce itself from any participation of government. Multicultural Ministries provided privilege for whatever culture involved to become an integral part of the United Pentecostal Church International. In this manner, people of multicultural distinction can be assimilated into the total function of the church and district, while guarding the legacy of language and culture.

Policies will continue to emerge that will allow future generations to work in harmony within the church family. The dynamics of the program is called: The One Church Concept. A concept of evangelism where the total community is evangelized and becomes one body, one church, one family, while still retaining the cultural identity of the people the church is targeting for evangelism.

The key so critical to successfully gaining entrance into the multicultural mind is culture— an element vital to the harmony of any evangelism program implemented. The reason behind this observation need go no further than the thoughts that relate to one's own love for his culture. And, those we are endeavoring to evangelize love their culture as much as we do. That is why the One Church Concept incorporates language and culture into an effective outreach program.

No compromise is to be expected from the cultural front, nor should any such demand be desired. The more we are aware that our objective is to evangelize the world— not to perpetuate an English organization—the less we will fight innovative ideas that will involve the total world's cultures in achieving the church's goal of world-evangelism.

Choosing between secular and spiritual values can involve dozens of variables— all interlocked to produce harmful delays in world evangelism.

Our priority is a successful program. Unique to the many efforts in Multicultural Ministries is the responsibility to fuse all cultures into an integral part of the United Pentecostal Church International—not a division of it.

Another key factor that comes into play is the homeland of the minority language groups we reach with the gospel. Their families are scattered on the mountainsides of some remote part of the world.... in the deep inaccessible valleys of a rain forest.... or behind some impregnable barrier of world opinion factor not in tune with the gospel. The key is to reach their culture here, develop and train them in doctrine and godly principles, and allow urgency to send them to reach their families with an indigenous approach.

Even a cursory glance should convince any man who loves this gospel that a positive future in world evangelism will depend upon a successful program to the minority language groups of North America. For our more intimate concern, Los Angeles, New York, Vancouver, Miami, San Francisco and many other major cities of North America hold vast resources of cultural ability. These resources are capable of bringing world missions into a brand new focus.

When we were a much smaller organization, and problems in evangelism were less intricate and conventional methods could solve our adverse situations. But we are rapidly approaching a drastically changing world—changes that are countering world evangelism. The world we are reaching today is, by far, a different world than we were reaching even ten years ago. What we need now is a viable program that will greatly enhance our abilities.

One big step is to come to grips with a right attitude. Like time, we can set our clocks to any desired hour convenient to personal activities, but setting the clock is not the deciding factor of time. All the preconceived ideas together, no matter how ingenious, will not determine the outcome of God's divine will in this matter.

The advantage of the broad program we are considering for Multicultural Ministries is decidedly clear. Allow me to belabor this point: Jesus became the author of this strategy many years ago. He said to the healed demoniac of Gadara, "Go home and tell thy friends..." In other words, go tell your own people. As a result, cities were impacted by His message. This is the idiosyncrasy of our plan. He was of another culture, even perhaps of another language, yet interwoven into an outreach of evangelism.

Some will cry out that the cost of additional evangelism programs is too great! We need to educate every negative mind that costs fall into two categories: direct financial outlay and the loss of what could have been gained had not programs been delayed. The truth of the matter is, if we would devote a greater share of our finances to evangelize the same people domestically we are now targeting in world missions, greater dividends would be gained. We could then share with our Foreign Missions Divisions revenue far more effective than finance— men.

Emerging techniques that have been put to work in the Western District since 1986 have given continuous growth to that district, both in the number of constituents of an existing church, and new churches being established. Success always speaks louder than failure, and a workable plan is easier to explain than a faltering scheme. This plan will work!

The promotion of Multicultural Ministries can be crucial! If we present it as a support ministry for our pastors, a reaction from those who tend to be fearful will have less capability to side track it before it can serve its purpose. Many times great programs are wrecked because a reaction was provoked. The basic principle is that we want bottom line results— not mere short-term victories. Therefore, we must determine our objectives by defining well the ultimate goal of Multicultural Ministries, and allow it to quietly make a big difference.

We can use our past experiences as a guide, but if any of our options are not being accepted we must brainstorm until we come up with a plan that will minimize static. Ripple effect of any activity that is implemented must not be neglected. If one action does not produce exactly what is needed or it triggers a host of problems, it must be returned to the drawing board for a quality that will become paramount to our objective. At any rate, a second strategy would be good to hold in reserve should the first falter. We fail only if we remain married to a program that is not working.

Since we are dealing with probabilities rather than absolutes, the yardstick for measuring our performance will be how the constituency is accepting our program. There is a long way to go between understanding in theory the workability of a plan, and being able to implement it in actual situations. Implementation can be very difficult when confronting men who have doubts concerning new ideas. In short, we need to start with little things, have our answers in focus by achievements—and build from there.

By maintaining a well informed public we have taken a giant step forward in eradicating all opposition to our initiative. With every step forward, the responsibility to our constituency increases. When we are quick to inform, the truth becomes evident that there is nothing to hide. Therefore, each cultural advance should be reported regularly in order that district officials and pastors maintain an upbeat attitude.

In every situation we must address issues openly. Pastors must work closely together with their leadership to identify any problem, and then unite to solve it. The future is too important, and time too essential, to do otherwise.

A cooperative relationship of both multicultural leaders and pastors must strive to discover what events and ideas cause an irritation, and move to modify the program accordingly. The total constituency then becomes recipient of the benefits.

When problem solving begins, we must understand that there is no such thing as a perfect situation. What may work in one area may not be so successful in another. It is only with complete unity and candor that all possible contributions to a problem should be explored. When strategy for dealing with a problem backfires, we should merely move to another perspective, desiring only that the Multicultural Ministries program succeed.

The interest and involvement of pastors will make a tremendous difference. And, there are many ways for local churches to participate. Through such active involvement we get a "feel" for the weakness, as well as the strengths, of this program.

Being involved in Multicultural Ministries will make a positive contribution to local church growth. If we become frightened and frustrated because we have to work our way through situations we will find ourselves filled with envy when we see other denominations reap our fields and carry our grain to their barns.

Therefore every one involved in Multicultural Ministries should encourage their peers to be firmly behind this program. Since finance will be necessary to its logistical structure, a firm step forward is to be willing to invest in the plan. George Washington, in early August of 1774, suggested that the colonial family resist British oppression by force. When those involved asked the key question, "How do you propose to do that?", he thundered, "I will raise one thousand men at my own expense and march to the relief of Boston." [1] The rest is history! Willingness to back a project sometimes calls for a sacrifice.

Sitting on our back doorstep are some of the very people God has commissioned us to go to other nations to evangelize... we must not allow the opportunity to pass. The forthcoming chapters will expose many areas pertinent to cross-culture evangelism. Let us investigate both the possibilities and the responsibilities to determine if the time is right to perpetuate the spirit our Lord injected into the program from the beginning.

Then, let's get to work....we know more about this business of evangelism than anyone in the world! But we are also more sensitive to the negatives it presents than we care to admit. There will be obvious tensions and strong nationalistic tendencies that will lobby for separation but we must persevere, confront, and solve tension, thereby defeating the devil in his attempt to delay our decisions. Strong leadership will be necessary to guide the assimilation process, but successes will pay great dividends. The solution is in our hands and time is not on our side. The one thing that should drive us to act is that today is not yesterday.

Footnotes:

[1] Immigration - Diversity in the U.S. - Leon F. Bouvier - Walker and Company

Chapter Two
Whose World Are We Evangelizing?

The church is not a place, it is people. Yet it is something more as well, it is a happening. Church is what happens when the people meet together with God. Singing, praying, preaching, giving, and receiving-all are means to an end. The church is where order is brought out of chaos; where hope replaces despair. Consequently, systematic changes must be made to apprehend advantages offered by opportunity. Moreover, emerging leaders must be taught to become sensitive to changes that are made necessary by differences in people, culture, and particular needs.

Because language is one of our most prevalent needs, and much frustration is a product of trying to overcome understanding barriers, the church must be a place where people feel free of impediment. Many people are lacking in understanding, not only of language and customs in our dominant society, but of a common biblical education. There are other cultures that have a totally different perspective of "religion". Much of North America's new society is involved in ancestor worship, reincarnation, and a myriad of characteristics void of understanding relative to the God of our fathers. Our leaders who occupy positions of authority must come to grips that these people are a part of the commission Jesus committed to the church.

The history of the United Pentecostal Church demonstrates a strong concern for world evangelism; a concern that has sent missionaries around the world to share the gospel message. Those concerns should never be relaxed. But the Lord of the Harvest realizes that the church is racing the rapture with millions yet unevangelized in the world. He has merely moved the people of the commission's purpose to the church's proximity to make the task easier.

Every church must be a missionary church. While the word "missionary" has been a term formally synonymous with "overseas" activity, today's church is faced with a backyard filled with the same cultures. (This is a positive argument for a growing percentage of money generally designated for missions being allocated locally.) Today's local assembly is a church where every member may become a "missionary" without leaving the local community. This type of evangelism depends upon an understanding of another's culture, new strategy, and an adjusted mentality.

Today's church must focus on God's vision for tomorrow rather than recreating yesterday, no matter how dramatic the history. Therefore, the real challenge facing this generation is change. Creativity and flexibility to meet opportunity is critical for there is a very large part of the world's diverse cultural entities now residing within reach of the North American pulpit.

It is necessary that people understand how important it is to evangelize immigrants with a fervor missionaries in foreign areas manifest toward the subjects of their calling. Neither the people nor the responsibility differ in principle. Many such immigrants will return to their own countries in time, perhaps to become key leaders in their society. How sad it would be to allow such an opportunity to pass undetected. Good churches are becoming unproductive because of a refusal to change set patterns and evangelism strategies designed for a past generation. The importance of creating loving and caring relationships with these visitors to our country can hardly be overstressed.

What if the church became sensitive toward the growing number of people moving into our neighborhoods from all over the world? The influx of these new residents- for whatever reason- is evident; not only in metropolitan areas, but throughout the rural United States and Canada as well. Never in North American history has the church had a greater opportunity as disciples of Jesus Christ to fulfill the mandate of its mission in the world. It boils down to change; a change in attitude, and a change in evangelism strategy. It is indispensable that our loyalty to Jesus Christ overcome the secular loyalty to culture, and pride of nationalism.

Any reluctance to adjust methodology in evangelism will not prevent God from doing the work that must be done. As in times past, He will merely step over unwillingness and provide others to meet the needs of a new generation. In short, He will evangelize the world with us or without us; the mission being greater than those performing it. Therefore the question to consider is, will the church fight to retain outmoded strategies because they worked so well a decade ago, or will it allow God to transform technique for the task at hand? I believe there is a definite need to focus upon the new mission frontiers that are before us.

God is calling upon us to adjust our methods in order to accomplish our task. We must welcome change in logistics, while retaining changeless principles of doctrine; value traditions we have long established while we continue to modify strategy. We must allow our congregations to be truly amiable toward new faces-especially those from other lands and cultures. We can only open the understanding of others by being open ourselves. We change people by changing ourselves as we come to realize that the earth is the Lord's and the fullness thereof, not just our corner of it.

Our engagement with the reformers must be for the long-term. However difficult things might be in the short-run, we must develop a faith in the strategic course we have set-reaching every culture residing in the United States and Canada- as the correct one.

In 1977, the United Pentecostal Church was deeply pondering the need to evangelize the variegated multicultural groups residing- legally and illegally- in the United States. Among the so called "ethnic" peoples were cultures whose forefathers had walked upon the land for several generations before the Anglo entered the same area as "newcomers". That those who walked these shores had taken it from others in times past was not the issue, for one wrong does not condone another, even as in future days the principle could work in the favor of another stronger than the present people.

Much has changed since the beginning efforts of Multicultural Ministries were implemented. Jack DeHart, a man with a burden to reach all cultures, was appointed as the coordinator of Ethnic Ministries. He played a key role in building and maintaining a viable program of evangelism to reach into the cultural pockets of North America with an excellence.

It was not easy to convince people who had lost self-esteem, felt as strangers in the land of their forefathers, and who were dedicatedly suspicious of any effort in their behalf that they were sincerely wanted in the predominantly white, English speaking North American church. But with a sensitive, intelligent, enthusiastic thrust, and a continuous interaction with the leaders of these cultures, poise and confidence won. A friendly, professional structure initiated a successful beginning that has become one of the stars in the banner of the United Pentecostal Church.

Multicultural Ministries was a necessary virtue for the United Pentecostal Church from the beginning. Was she to be truly an international church, or was she to be a spiritual business endeavor with branch offices scattered throughout the world? If she was to be truly international, she could not ignore that both benefits and responsibilities be shared by her successes. Neither could she spend millions extending the borders of her endeavors on foreign soils, keeping the results of her labors at the end of fearful finger-tips, and ignore the same cultures living within the sound of domestic pulpits. She decided that she was truly international in scope as well as name, and Multicultural Ministries became a credible program.

As the Annual General Conference attracted its congregation from around the world, the landscape became a new world. Suddenly a transformation began to come into focus, new dreams were embraced, new visions made necessary adjustments to the mechanism, and leaders were touched with compassion. The result began to form a mosaic pattern in the General Conference as multicultural constituents became delegates to the conference.

Jack DeHart felt to give more of his time to the emerging Church Growth structure, an area of ministry proven by his many books on the subject. Over my spirited protest he remained committed to his choice to resign as Ethnic Ministries coordinator. As Spanish Ministries coordinator, I had worked loyally at his side, and the advances effectuated by the Spanish had signaled a spill-over into other cultural language groups. Since total harmony reigned among the Spanish ministers and they had proven there was to be no division mentality, but rather a total synthesizing of believers, it was decided that a "one church" mentality was to be the principle upon which all multicultural ministries should be constructed. It was decided that I should be appointed to provide continuity for this important program. There was broad approval expressed by the multicultural brethren due to my missionary years in South America, influencing the program to become mercuric as new fronts were initiated in many parts of the country. The dynamics were in place, and the structure of organized evangelism was established, so why shouldn't the ministry expand?

Committees were called together to provide direction for long-term goals. Special task forces removed stigmas of the past with innovative answers for difficult questions that had plagued assimilation. Barriers were removed and the fears of cultural prejudice suddenly dissipated in the minds of many who had been skeptical. Color lines slowly were not as visible as they once had been, and the word minority ceased to be a buzz-word. Even the word "ethnic" lost its importance as the ministry replaced it with "the family." Suddenly cultural Family Camps took shape and were successful. Seminars were taught to educate the English white pastors of the possibilities, and at the same time in-depth studies by district officials and revered cultural personnel produced knowledgeable leaders for the emerging ministries. This increased the options for a truly effective program of evangelism. Widespread recognition for cultural acceptance impacted multilingual areas until at present 15 distinct cultural groups have been organized and are being effectively incorporated into the North American church. With many of our major cities appearing more and more as a miniature world, success can only be expected.

At a time when racial prejudice has taken a more subtle turn and where relations between cultural groups have in more times than not dipped to an explosive level, the church world should stand head and shoulders taller than the secular. Hope should replace despair, and joy should elevate the soul of all living creatures to an unprecedented stature. To reflect the scriptures, the church shall be a body where there is neither Jew nor Greek, bond or free. The church is the sum of the total among all the cultures of the world, simply because it is the body of Jesus Christ reconciling all men to God.

The greatest basic principle makeup of Christian character is courtesy-good manners. The difference between a firm commitment to principle and rudeness many times is mere a fine line. The attitude that is displayed will determine the depth of commitment and the courage to follow that which is right. One first of all defends a value by practicing it, and that with a courtesy that speaks louder than verbal activity. While the church family must not be afraid to defend the right to denounce racial prejudice and exclusiveness, it must do so with a courtesy that displays right principles. Reverse prejudice can also grow into a misdirected attack that creates more division than it solves. That goes for all cultures, not just the dominant. All cultures must stand for the principles that produce right motives, as the family of God strives to stamp out the many little things that disturb harmony. The secular world has its rhetoric to openly promote issues that relate to culture. However, the church is a different matter. We are one family, and one body. When we were born again, we were born into a family where we have one Father. That makes all believers brothers and sisters in the family. We must have a natural feeling about respect for race, and if there are problems of racial nature, it must be the other person's problem. There are many more areas where we agree than where we disagree. We must focus upon the big picture and the positive rewards of our perseverance, not on a few minor points that irritate. That advice is good for all people, no matter the culture to which they belong.

Secularly, the United States is- sometimes in practice, often in ideology, and always in makeup- the first global nation. Again we as a church must address the difficulties that accompany such an endeavor. There are those who preach separatism. God preaches a united body. Take the Black-White cultural issue for example. Those who push for separatism on both sides of the question have never understood that "America" did not hate Blacks. In the secular sense, many Americans did, and still do. But not the country as a whole. This principle is easily defended by the events of the Civil War battlefields where many fought- and died- to bring an end to the ghastly slavery issue. Therefore keeping the perspective will require a balance between cultural diversity and commitment to the church. Not only must we eradicate prejudice emanating from the dominant society against any and all of God's creation, but from the reverse side as well. We must be foremost and always the church, with a love that transcends all barriers, and that with an understanding from whatever culture given the privilege to be a part. Simmering anger between people will only threaten any future God will provide us, no matter how subtle it may be presented. Cultural hatred must come to an abrupt end!

It is time to educate this generation to introduce the next with open minds and understanding hearts. We must be a church with the courage to match our convictions, and the will to define them. While it is the secular right of all men to establish values for themselves the church must establish the fact that all ideas and lifestyles are not equal. Some lifestyles are right and some are wrong. We must not permit the wrong to impose their values upon those of our charge. However, where cultural values do not conflict with biblical principle, we should not impose cultural values of a dominant society upon another culture as a test of acceptance. If the church does not function within its walls to eradicate inequality by tearing down cultural barriers then how will it testify to the secular world of the peace and harmony the scripture promises to believers?

Our world has the possibility to explode with promise as we accept the daily challenges relative to culture. Can you imagine the happy air of cross-racial, cross-cultural camaraderie among teens as they champion the cause of a new world where Christ can be preached without barrier? Where stereotypes have been dropped from the rhetoric of the righteous? What about racial jokes that illicit mirth when directed toward those of another culture, language, or color? How is it that freedom to stereotype is perfectly acceptable until it happens to enter a two-way street. Yes, our world will find new hopes and realize new dreams if those who evangelize it will fine-tune the process.

We can make the world better with some badly needed adjustments; as many in our own attitude as those of another. The objective would stimulate critical thinking and frankness until an acceptable balance is achieved. It is in struggle we will define ourselves and call upon conviction and courage to infuse into converts who will one day fight and win the battles we could not.

Persecution? Opposition? Sure, there will be plenty of it. Persecution, sometimes severe- sometimes mild- has always affected the patterns of evangelism. Do we expect it to be otherwise? But it will not stop the church.

Neither should the church think in terms of controls that radiate ownership. We must begin thinking of churches multiplying around the world, not as a branch of, or an extension of a dominant culture, but of world evangelism as the great commission is fulfilled.

Too many problems? Many of the church's problems have nothing to do with evangelism. But when evangelism becomes the greater priority, it will be surprising how many problems on the periphery will have found their solution.

Many misgivings have emerged because a massive cultural transformation is forcibly changing evangelism methods in North America. This attitude has come about in part because people of such varied backgrounds have begun to fuse themselves into the fellowship, and a feeling of displacement is suffered by the established membership. However, when the cause of the gospel has come into sharp focus, the majority of these difficulties disappear. When changes have been contemplated carefully by a dominant culture, it usually brings diversity into a splendorous beauty where the values of all involved are fused to add luster and distinction.

The Reader's Digest had an article intended for humor that tells the story best. Life in these United States spoke of Joseph Spencer of Miami,

Florida, pushing his shopping cart through the aisles of a supermarket as he shopped for a Fourth of July picnic. His cart bumped another being pushed by a Hispanic man. Joseph Spencer spoke no Spanish, and the other shopper spoke no English, so apologies were exchanged through smiles.

Joseph Spencer looked into the other's shopping cart- hot dogs, hamburgers, rolls, potato chips, ketchup and coleslaw. His new found friend followed his eyes and motioned to the cart Joseph was pushing. They both burst out laughing as the contents contained selected tortillas, avocados, chili peppers and refried beans.[1] A true picture of change in the secular world. In fact culinary polls have discovered that Mexican food is now the favorite of the North American appetite.

On the spiritual side of the coin millions of Hispanic Americans have left the Roman Catholic Church. From store-front churches in urban slums to the gleaming structures along suburban freeways, perhaps as many as 5 million of the 42 million Hispanics living legally in the United States now attend a worship center apart from their traditional catholic heritage. The move is accelerating with such speed that somewhere impacts will be made.

The thousands who leave the church daily are attracted by the influence of friends and relatives who have experienced a living relationship with God that contrasts the boredom of the ritualism of Catholicism. They are learning that a church service can have real meaning, and not be just a ceremony.

The new immigrants, the Asians, are coming from religious histories as variegated as the number of cultures they represent. Family unity among them many times is threatened as the younger Asian embraces Christianity. The elderly is a person who has long been steeped in ancestor worship, reincarnation, as firm Buddhists, Shintoists, Taoism, and a myriad of other backgrounds where a living God is not the central figure. All of this tends to place a greater responsibility upon the church, for these precious souls are a part of the world the church is commissioned to evangelize.

Santeria, a religion of the Caribbean with its roots in Africa and Cuba, mixes animal sacrifices- barnyard variety- and spiritual communication to fabricate a very complex form of worship. When slaves from Africa were brought to Cuba, they masked the orishas as Roman Catholic saints. Today, Santeria, meaning "way of the saints," is a combination of the original African beliefs and Catholicism. Sacrifice to the orishas is central to Santeria. Sometimes the appearances are very similar to voodoo or satanism, and has characteristics of the occult. Practiced mainly by the Haitian's and the Cubans, it has presented serious problems for the Christian family, as well as a concern for the legal community. The influx of many diverse religions of the world into North America has been a formidable tool to diminish the influence of Christianity, and turn our immigrants away from truth. This will always be a challenge, but with diligence we can turn every attack into victory. It will be done by the way we display our attitude toward those who are culturally different, and it will be done because we are what we are, and who we are-we are the church!

The question is not whether these new Americans can be assimilated into the fellowship- they must be- but how the church will be changed by the process. For the United Pentecostal Church the responsibility of cultural diversity has come to rest upon the shoulders of Multicultural Ministries. By being involved with each particular grouping, this ministry is to be the bridge that will communicate the values ultimately woven into the overall fabric. Harmony of thought results as biblical principles emerge as guidelines to a personal relationship with Jesus Christ.

Multicultural Ministries has served the United Pentecostal Church International well in this regard. It has brought understanding to the body as the changing face of evangelism reaps the rich, golden harvest merely waiting to be apprehended. This change has the characteristics that could facilitate the mechanism of the church toward a revolution for world evangelism, and a fulfilling of the great commission.

This is an issue that will be faced now, or it will be faced in eternity where the church will answer a most significant question from the throne-why not? If a church does not see itself as an aggressive, evangelistic church which desires to mirror God's love to His creatures- all of them- it could become an ineffective clanking of machinery after the lubrication is gone, dying of its own activity. It has lost its purpose for existing.

Our destiny is not to remain as we are, but move on to what we must become. If we are to bring new believers to a living faith in Christ Jesus, it will require new dynamics to meet new opportunities. Now is the time to move boldly. The task of the ages- world evangelism- behooves us to make the necessary adjustments to accomplish it. The challenge before us is to reestablish purpose and direction immediately while the opportunities abound around us.

When we acquire a stark vision of the world destined for judgment unless we can reach it with the gospel, evangelism will actually explode from within! We must become committed .....and that today! Our churches of this hour have the opportunity to provide the world a preview of heaven. What a beautiful sight when around our local altars the redeemed of all nationalities, people, and tongues worship. We have made it happen as a result our love for the gospel. It has happened, because as a church we have fulfilled the commission, in our communities and around the world. When we went forth to evangelize the whole world, every creature... not just our kind, we evangelized HIS world. The end-result will be recorded in Revelations 7.

Footnotes:

[1] Readers Digest, July 1993

Chapter Three
The Church's Purpose

"But if a stranger sojourn with. thee in your land, ye shall not vex him.. But the stranger that dwelleth with you shall be unto you as one. from among you, and. thou shalt love him as thyself; for ye were strangers in the land of Egypt: I am the Lord your God."
Leviticus 19: 33-34

      The Church provides a refuge for a weary, sin tossed world. Sinners, tired of the grief given birth by the many upheavals of a lifestyle void of God, find peace within its walls. For it is there that happiness replaces depression and singing drives the tears far from eyes accustomed to weeping. This is a common story among believers who long have possessed a background of a saving Christ, but only recently in North America have countless others been introduced to His saving grace.

      Today the United Pentecostal Church is enjoying a growth of a new generation of believers. They too, have found new life, and the fabulous truth they have embraced includes a complete change from everything they have ever known! They are the Asians who in the past worshiped gods many, including lifeless images formed of inanimate materials. Their lifestyle also involved ancestor worship where family traditions had no intimacy nor interest in a crucified Christ.

      Just as the church becomes a melting pot of a cross-section of humanity emerging from many denominational traditions, the United Pentecostal Church is experiencing a great revival sweeping the west coast. This revival is resulting in a complete change of face from the accepted norm of yesterday's results. Demographic changes constantly altering set patterns have influenced greatly the genetic amalgamation taking place. It is not surprising to hear several languages as the sounds of prayer fill a local church sanctuary. Neither is it surprising to see representatives of as many as four or five cultures who have already assimilated into the spiritual family, assisting a new convert in the altar, each worshipping in the language of his birth.

      The principle boils down to accepting cultural ambiguities into the local assembly. The gospel is Jesus Christ! It is the essence of His principle and love. He became the foundation of faith that produces quality and character in the life of an individual. Living by the standards He taught brings not only the joy and peace necessary for the normal existence in the present, but a platform upon which to build a security for eternity. It was for this reason Jesus commissioned his disciples to spread the gospel, "Take my principles to EVERY creature in my world..." It is, therefore, the responsibility of the disciples, and the discipled, to put into practice that which will produce a continual cycle of spiritual reproduction.

The commission's specifics of "every creature" give direction to go beyond the boundaries of the language and culture of the believer, even beyond the boundaries of national government, with the gospel.

The responsibility to evangelize the world increases with the explosive rate of population growth. Today, even with the rising interest in world missions and the sacrificial giving that sends men with the purpose of preaching Christ to the world, there is still much to do. Utilizing present methods, it is possible that the end will come before the task is complete. With eyes focused upon lengthening shadows of evening-time, there is an increasing urgency upon the church to reach the world with the gospel. Frustration appeals to God for assistance in this cause, and he responds with an explanation, "Since you have not gone....sent....or made sufficiently possible the success of taking the gospel to the whole world, I will bring the whole world to the gospel." Could it be that immigration has been utilized by our God to enhance the fulfillment of the commission?

Some of God's activity in this regard has caused men to cry out in protest. They see personal interests threatened, and look on the natural side of things, and immigration as merely an intrusion of foreigners into our country. God sees it as the Creator who is merely providing the gospel for His world. It was He who regulated the division of nations and people into diverse language and custom at the Tower of Babel. He is bringing it back together by a tremendous Pentecost capable of uniting language and culture into one body-the church. It is after all still HIS world! He motivates people to bring about the greatest degree of results for his divine purpose and kingdom. I see a historical parallel re-occurring time and again as He brings men into an encounter with the message of salvation. He further taught this principle in the law as He urged His people to minister to immigrants as "strangers within the gates."

Lord, who is the stranger that we may treat him kindly? To whom were you referring when you spoke your searing rebuke, I was hungry.... you gave me no meat. I was naked..... you clothed me not. I was a stranger..... you took me not in! Evident was the surprise reflected upon those hearing your words to the extent they cried. Lord, when have we seen you naked.....hungry ....a stranger? Then it slowly dawns upon us that you could come into your world.... as a stranger.

God has constantly brought empty hearts to the fountains of salvation to send them away again full and satisfied. He uses circumstances to produce logical reasons for motivation. During the potato famine of the 1840s, hundreds of thousands of Irishmen left their homeland. An act of God brought them face to face with a decision; stay and face possible starvation, or become a member of a new society. America, produced by God to become the exporter of the gospel-a hotbed of evangelism-received the "stranger" who would as a result experience an encounter with the gospel.

The stranger in American evolution became a part of her heritage, and relatively few are those who cannot point to a background of people willing to work hard, and who refused to accept a handout for "free". They were a people who contributed much to the building of the Union Pacific Railroad and assisted in the advancement of the American frontier. But until roots were firmly lodged in American soil, they were the stranger in the gates. Their children became us; and in the church became strong advocates of the gospel.

We must not forget the African blood that ran free in the homeland of their birth. What a great price they paid for their drink at the spiritual fountain. While the decision was not by personal choice to come into the proximity of the gospel, none the less the encounter was made. By the time history had brought the Black to a prominent place, the gospel had become a great part of their life. Very few can sing about Jesus out of the soul as can the Black. Their song was born to sustain them, for during the time of slavery only by experiencing salvation in Jesus Christ were they free.

Italy, Hungary, Austria, and Germany followed the migration trail during the closing years of the 1800s with such activity that nearly 27 percent of America's population was of that bloodline. Because of political upheaval they searched for a new home, and became strangers entering the gates. Each lent talent, stamina and character to the system as they made up what we know today as America, the land of the free…

War brings havoc to any society, and always results in displacement of people. With homes destroyed and families suffering disaster, hope is kindled to move to a place of security. In each case in history, the United States and Canada have maintained open doors to receive the oppressed. Take a look at more recent events; Korea, Vietnam, Laos, and as a result of the cold war, Russia. As the results of war, political upheaval, and economics bring people into focus with American society, a question is posed, "How effective has our world evangelism been to their spiritual need?" Yet now, new and innovative programs are at work for these people who are "strangers" among us. Pastors are coming to grips with problems of language ambiguity, cultural differences, and taking time to look beyond the fearful threats posed by infusing believers into a multi-cultural congregation. It is more specifically defined as being sensitive to God's direction, and responding to a need of all of God's creation to have an opportunity to hear the gospel.

We have our Foreign Mission's program that sends men to many quarters of the world. This is what the church was commissioned to do, but is there a difference because they have come to us? Immigration of the world's cultures into our neighborhoods emanates opportunity! The grain has come to the proximity of the garner. The stranger has come within our gates to provide a more effective program of evangelism. They have become our business; our responsibility.

Today, since Spanish represents the world's third largest language grouping, the Master of the Harvest is bringing the crop to us. He is creating circumstances that are motivating the Spanish community to come to the fountain. We, as God's children, must understand the purpose, and not frustrate the cause. We must keep our priorities in the realm of the spiritual. When we reach Spanish people with the gospel, we will be able to disciple them and send them to the Spanish world, both near and far, within this nation and outside these boundaries. They will increase the effectiveness of the gospel by giving it credibility of language proficiency and cultural awareness. They will reproduce Pentecost by sharing with their own "in the tongue in which they were born". In this manner the needs of the Spanish world can be better met.

In the case of political and philosophical differences in the world, there are many cultures closed to the representatives of the gospel. Missionaries unable to penetrate the barriers of legal opposition must stand idly by as the world behind the barrier dies without God. The influx of that culture into North America, and coming in contact with the gospel, provides a new opportunity never before afforded the church. Multicultural Ministries is there to provide the gospel, and the gospel having accomplished its redeeming work in the heart, provides the church with a missionary that can go legally beyond the barrier to witness the great love of God to that people.

As we consider these facts before us in the light of "strangers within the gates," who is the person among us possessing knowledge of the heritage of America, that is not forced to realize the truth? That while we can look back with pride at the accomplishments our ancestry has made upon this land we call America, it did not begin there. We are forced to jump across oceans to lands far away; to lands with as many names as there are countries in the world, and admit that at some point in America's evolving history, we were the strangers within the gates! Check with blushing faces those of us who have attempted to bar entrance, or have complained as a result of hardship, or realized any threat that might present itself. The investigation of our past will reveal that our ancestry originated in another country and through opened doors were finally fused into mainstream America. It is then more than probable that because of this we were subjected to the gospel and became what we are. Therefore the task is before us to bend our backs to the load, sacrificing time and effort, along with our finances, to bring the commission into sharp focus for those who are now strangers. To give thanks to God for His making our responsibility to the gospel easier by

His special efforts in bringing the world to us.

Since my main objective is the ethnic cultures of our world, I cry out in their behalf! "For the Lord your God is a God of gods, and Lord of lords, a great God, a mighty, and a terrible, which regardeth not persons, nor taketh reward: He ....loveth the stranger, in giving him food and raiment. Love ye therefore the stranger: for ye were strangers....." Deuteronomy 10:17-19

To give a special insight by illustration, recently a young Cantonese lady, Judy Quach gave her heart to the Lord in El Monte, California. Barely able to understand English, she reverted to Cantonese in order to feel liberty in worship. She attended the Western District Ladies' Retreat, yearning desperately to be filled with a Holy Ghost she had been taught was a gift from God. One evening during her faithful appeals in the altar, she turned to a sister praying by her side. "I didn't know you could speak Cantonese!' She happily exclaimed in her broken English. The sister smiled, "I don't speak any language other than English." She replied. "But... all during the time I was praying, you were encouraging me in Cantonese, and instructing me!" Judy insisted. God is capable of supplying all our needs, even capability to speak languages other than our own as a sign to searching hearts.

Judy received the Holy Ghost that night because God departed from the normal and inserted the necessary ingredient so direfully needed.

Peter Ton was evangelized by his friend, Ba Quach, also of El Monte. Today Peter leads the devotions each evening as El Monte UPC membership lifts its variegated heart to God. Both Ba and Peter, who are of Chinese descent, were refugees from Vietnam, arriving in California after horrifying experiences throughout the long journey. However, you'd never have that impression now, with Ba playing the keyboard, and Peter behind the pulpit manifesting the very love of God extended to whomsoever will.

Thongdee Somsack, a real live wire from Stockton, California, is committed to evangelism. His testimony never fails to thrill the heart of the hearer. He was very unhappy with his first visit to a Pentecostal service. Since the greatest part Asians are a more reserved culture, the emotional impact of a dynamic Pentecostal environment was too much. "I felt there was nothing for me there...." he once confided in me. He went home, but could not get the service out of his mind, and felt drawn to return for unexplainable reasons. When he did return, it was to give God his life, and he was ultimately filled with the Holy Ghost and baptized in Jesus name. Not surprisingly, "Toney" now reacts to the same emotions that once repelled him. Today, he has come into a living relationship with God, and his life is synonymous to his faith.

His father was understandably distressed. Toney was leaving the traditions of generations! He was very severe, but Toney was committed. "I'm sorry, father, that you feel this way, but when you come to know Him, you will understand." Toney's father did come to know Jesus, and consequently his family is now in the church. This is only one experience among many where a departure from family traditions and eastern religions has brought strain upon a family relationship. As soul winners, we sometimes fail to understand that there are backgrounds that are completely void of the Christian faith. God will help us to cross those barriers, but we must comprehend the tremendous battle that wages in the heart of these people. People like Toney are emerging as very productive leaders among United Pentecostal Asians.

Calvary Tabernacle of Sacramento, California, serves a spiritual banquet of diversity every Sunday. Beginning at 8:00 AM, the Hmong community-every one a bonafide member of Calvary-have their worship. 10:00 AM introduces Black evangelism, and at 1:00 PM, the Russians pack the building far beyond capacity, preaching a one God, baptized in Jesus name, Spirit filled message. The Russian congregation is in excess of four hundred holy living, Bible believing constituents. The mother church congregation enters at 4:30 PM for a service that has the appearance of heaven's church of Revelations due the many cultures attending, and at 7:30 PM, the Spanish have their service. When the Holy Ghost falls, as it frequently does, the entering congregation merely merges into the action to participate in the spiritual smorgasbord being served.

I was privileged to be involved in Calvary's services recently. I attended each, and spoke during three of the five services. There was such a feeling of liberty that I stood amazed. Each service was crowned by God's divine presence, and several received the Holy Ghost. No one was hurried, and there was no fear that time would be limited. Oh, how beautiful it was!

In the principle service of the evening, a mass choir was presented. I counted seven cultures that made up the powerful sound of music that resulted. I wept at the very sight! Singing? Friend, they sang that night until the very building seemingly trembled with excitement.

There is a preview of heaven displayed around our United Pentecostal Church altars as our many variegated cultures worship the God of all mankind. The Western District through Multicultural Ministries is evangelizing the same cultures our missionaries abroad are reaching, and have full expectation that revival fires will be ignited that will spread to regions beyond like a raging inferno. With many language groups now being touched by Multicultural Ministries, why not?

Chapter Four
Immigrants, Or Future In The Making?

Multicultural Ministries is the answer to world evangelism. When it appeared as though the church had reached its limitation due the population explosion around the globe, suddenly God brought secular strength into the program. He took the American Dream syndrome that inspired cultures from all over the world to come to America, and with a master stroke of ingenious proportions, incorporated immigration into evangelism. Given the fact that the first-world exists only a mere five minute walk across land from the third-world along its southwest border of the United States, or a few minutes flight time from many major airports, immigration could provide the necessary ingredient for an effective evangelism program. Immigrants from innumerable countries and cultures merely by coming to the United States and Canada are evangelized, and the result translated to tremendous advances in world evangelism.

Many times secular America places all the blame for its immigration problems upon illegal migration, but many times there were other more subtle methods at work. For the benefit of demonstrating how effective immigration can be to end-time revival, please allow me to walk with you through the many reasons for immigration, those who were responsible, and those it affected. Balance this with the possibilities provided by a powerful world evangelism effectuated by reverse migration, and a more beautiful picture comes into focus. Also, a little background will provide a greater comprehension of this difficult perplexity. If you knew that immigration was perpetuated in the beginning, not by the immigrants, but for what benefit immigration could produce private industry, you might develop a more sympathetic attitude toward it. At least, if you could imagine it as a divine plan instituted to serve world evangelism.

I must not take sides with the immigration question except to champion the cause of evangelism. In this I do firmly believe the task of evangelizing the world will be made easier by the waves of immigration coming in contact with the North American church. In short the Master is saying to the church, "You are racing a setting sun with much of the world yet unreached. I am bringing the world to you."

The reasons for immigration are many as well as complex. But it is not a new problem. All of us were immigrants at one time- even the American Indian. It is generally believed that they probably came across a land bridge between Siberia and Alaska. While very little is known about the dangerous voyages these early immigrants undertook, they were, perhaps, motivated by the same desire for improved existence. Every American Indian folklore story includes the "Old Ones," meaning of course, those who were displaced by the coming of a new society, the Anasazi. Population became the survival of the fittest. The "Old Ones" disappeared, but without doubt under the layer of exterior culture of emerging times, could be found traces of the passing lineage. Then a new culture successfully assimilated them into an acceptable trait.

Much immigration took place before the Revolutionary War period. The war was fought in order that the colonists could break away from England. It is easy to forget that the colonists were also immigrants.

President Franklin Roosevelt, in a speech made to the Daughters of the American Revolution in the 1930s, addressed the delegates as "my fellow immigrants." He was emphasizing the point that all were immigrants.[1]

Reasons for immigration are numerous. However, one principle stands out as a major contribution-economics. People want a better life. The American Dream has produced a continual confidence that by immigrating to America, an opportunity to achieve a better life is guaranteed. Your daily newspapers will underline this as a primary reason.

Economic motives propel the Haitian who will risk his life in a leaky boat to reach the Florida coastline. Chinese swarmed to labor camps along the Union Pacific Railroad as they provided the necessary manpower to advance the rails. Mexican farm laborers crossed the borders of California and Texas to earn more money than they were able to earn in their country, and today that which is known as the new immigrant from Southeast Asia is perpetuating the dream.

Then there is the forced immigration during an era from which most Americans wish to hide their faces. It was the beginning of one of the most detestable periods of history when shipload after shipload of Africans were brought to the U.S. against their will. They were enslaved as a source of cheap labor for plantation owners in the southern colonies. Readily supplied by wealthy shipping companies from the northeast, slavery became a lucrative occupation for those who were involved on both sides of the coin. This displacement of persons forged a history that brought shame and indelible degradation as fellow humans labored under animalistic conditions. The immigrants numbered into the millions, and until it became a civil rights issue, the slave trade was given continuity.

Another factor not often mentioned as a factor is the infusion of "legal" Spanish workers recruited by the thousands to answer the demand for industrial laborers. This coupled with California's continual need for diversified agriculture, Colorado's sugar beet fields, Texas cotton fields, and New Mexico's copper mines. The northeast also placed a call for willing workers to work the iron foundries and the Appalachian coal mines.

The northern steel mills recruited Mexicans. In 1923 Bethlehem Steel brought approximately 1,000 Mexicans from Texas to act as 'strikebreakers' in its Bethlehem, Pennsylvania, plant. In the same year National Tube Company, an affiliate of United States Steel, recruited about 1,500

Mexicans for its Lorain, Ohio plant. That same year further involved Mexican laborers for the Illinois Steel Mills. They came willingly and legally, but established themselves in their new home. Between 1920 and 1930 Chicago's population of Mexican-Americans had expanded from 4,000 to nearly 20,000, making it the largest Spanish-speaking area in the United States outside the southwest.[2] Most of them continued to live within the shelter of their group culture in order to share familiar language and customs.

Political refugee status is often given many immigrants. Survival is at stake. There is fear of political terrorism, or even death. Even as Ethiopian farmers flee certain starvation, many Central Americans flee political terrorism.

Refugees are not a new problem. Many early American settlers were refugees from religious and political persecution in Europe. Some were forced to flee Great Britain because of their refusal to accept a state religion, while other early Americans left Germany because their political opinions were considered dangerous. The Irish were forced to find better conditions due the potato famine, and while each immigrant has his own story to tell, there seems to be no end to valid reason for immigration.

The displeasure of the older immigrant has always been manifested against the newer immigrant. Arguments that give one reason over another rarely solve the issue, since what was insufferable for one, became purpose for the other. The society of North America in 1776 was a very diverse one. The people represented many races, religions, and ethnic groups. They spoke different languages. They were the people upon which was constructed the society you and I know. We are the result.

Therefore, America is a country that endlessly re-invents itself, working the revision that turns "them" into "us". That is the American secret: motion, new combinations, absorption-a changing face. The process, while explosive, is also very unique. America is more than a nation, it is a world contained in a people. We are they, and because "they" came, we became "us". Yet because of this, the America of the world has become a dream to live in the minds of youth around the globe. The process has made America great!

The dynamic energy of new combinations is changing the United States today as profoundly as it did in colonial days. In the days of forced immigration of ten million Africans, or at the turn of the century in the luster-tinted days of Ellis Island. Those were the days when America became a blend of cultures so minutely that out of it rose a nation. A nation that while distinctly different from all others, it was strangely related to the rest of the entire world. It is upon this basis that Multicultural Ministries builds its case.

The faces involved in the change are different now-mostly brown or yellow. Twenty years ago, more than half of all immigrants came from Europe and Canada. Today, most are Mexicans, Filipinos, Vietnamese, Koreans, Asian Indians, Chinese, Salvadorans and Jamaicans. They scramble across the border near San Ysidro, California, in the middle of the night. They get off their jets and stream through customs at Kennedy Airport in New York. They arrive in the trunks of cars, or land at secluded beaches on the Florida Keys.

Native-born Americans are ambivalent about the new arrivals. Ambivalence is what old Americans have always felt about new Americans. At the removal of several generations from Ellis Island, some sentimentalize the immigrant experience. They project their nostalgia upon the new immigrant and wish him well. But the native-born also feels the alien vibration. Alien is a dank and sinister word-the ominous other-ness, not our kind. Racism in new combinations jumps the fences of the generation gap of those who have forgotten that "we" were the "they's" of yesterday, and those new Americans are those with faces of brown and yellow who have come to take away the jobs of the established. But established when... and how.... and by whom?

Americans alternate between hospitality and paranoia about newcomers, between promiscuous inclusiveness and indigenous recoil. It was different, they say, when the whole continent lay before us and needed building. The job is done. How long will it be before these newcomers from the third World overwhelm the "democratic" process, and a new, diverse ideology emerges? That's a good question.

But many times the memory is short-or was it lost in the retrospection of "we've never had it so good". If the backlash of resentment had prevailed in those days, how many of "us" would have never known the life we have today, or would we have ever come in contact with the genes that made us "us". Those who wished to turn back earlier waves of immigration sometimes used the same language, or worse.

In a sense, America long ago made a shrewd instinctive bargain with the world. It offered a prize-its wealth, its freedom and promise- and then dared those strong enough to take the leap. It was, and is a hard journey.

It was America, really, that got the prize: the enormous energy unleashed by the immigrant dislocations. Being utterly at risk, moving into a new and dangerous land, makes the immigrant alert and quick to learn. It stimulates reflexes, and produces adrenaline. The immigrant, uprooted, cannot take traditional nourishment from the prominence of home, of place, from an arrangement that existed before he existed, and would persist after he died. When you search for an American, you must cut away the layers of generation and see the rusty cinnamon of skin color and the rustic custom of a nomad. Everyone else is an immigrant with only time separating the event.

All of us are the ingredients of time, and the immigrant who travels in both time and geographical space becomes the fusion that produces change. The dimensions of time and space collaborate. America, a place, becomes time: the future.

When the truth becomes evident, there is nothing sinister about the immigrant. They work long hours and live for their children. Many are more serious about time than those known as the established. They contribute their bloodlines, their traditions and spirit to make America's vitality and uniqueness. They become "Americans". They become "us" and only the future of that time has a perception of "them".

The United States is an ongoing experiment to prove or disprove the theory that proclaims people who are culturally different can live together as one nation.[3]

The U.S. Census Report stated that the number of foreign-born people living in the United States has climbed to 20 million. This is important to know when planning evangelism outreach activities. Foreign-born means the individuals who have migrated as a first generation, and not to be confused with those who are of ethnic descent, but who have been born in the United States.

That demographic changes are drastically taking root is obvious by the changes in the school system. For students to be enrolled in every level of the education program, the fact is that parents have established themselves in the community. The children will melt into every thing the social system implies. Learning customs and culture, and eventually becoming proficient in English. This means the gospel can, in time, touch their lives. However, the fact is the home is a bilingual battle. The adults, without doubt, will continue to speak native tongues, while the children fight to become a part of their surroundings. The parents must be evangelized in their heart language.

Spanish and Mandarin Chinese are the most frequently spoken languages in the Los Angeles area. In the San Gabriel School District, 42 percent of the students who have another primary language speak Spanish and 31 percent speak one of five different Chinese dialects, including Mandarin.

In the Pasadena Unified District, 88 percent of the students with another first language speak Spanish, followed by Mandarin Chinese with 29 percent, Armenian with 7 percent and Tagalog (the native language of the Philippines) with one percent.

In Duarte, 86 percent of the students with another first language speak Spanish, but the diversity spans 36 languages, from Tagalog to Punjabi.

With 80 languages spoken in Los Angeles, how many others could we add to that number when additional cultures living in San Francisco,

New York, Miami, Vancouver are taken into consideration? The list is nearly endless!

Chinese, Filipinos, Indians and Koreans led an explosive growth in the nation's Asian-American population during the decade of the 1980s. The Chinese community more than doubled in size-to 1.6 million. The number of Filipinos grew by more than 80 percent, to 1.4 million. Inglewood High School, 90% white 20 years ago and 90% Black 10 years ago, is 48% Latino today. At the University of California, Berkeley, most entering freshmen say they were attracted to the school because of its cultural variety: there is no ethnic majority.

There, in a nutshell, is the story of California's ethnic landscape. As recently as 1980, California was 76% white. During the past ten years, the Hispanic community grew nearly 70%, the Asian community 127%, so that by the 1990 census, California was only 57% white. During this same period the white community grew by a mere 6%.[4] It is quite clear that early on, the time will come when there will be no clear racial majority at all. California is, by any measure, America's most colorful state as it relates to ethnicity.

More specifically, a sizable chunk of the nearly 5 million immigrants who came to America between 1985 and 1990 call the San Gabriel Valley home. The San Gabriel Valley lies just east of the city of Los Angeles, and has become the epitome of ethnic population growth in the United States.

Monterey Park placed fifth among the nation's cities which have large numbers of immigrants, with 51.8 percent of its 62,000 residents foreign born. This influx of immigrants made Monterey Park the first Asian-majority city on the U.S. mainland. This middle-class city went from being 14 percent Asian in 1970 to 56 percent Asian-mostly Chinese-in 1990. The secret of cultural harmony in Monterey Park is that all parties involved have tried to demonstrate that all cultures can indeed exist side by side. They step in quickly to handle tension and conflict.[5]

The Asian group to carefully monitor is not the Japanese or the Chinese we have come to accept, but the Filipinos. They are growing at an astronomical rate. Koreans follow close behind. Other Valley cities with large first-generation immigrant populations include El Monte and Rosemead, each with 48 percent.

Further the bureau reported that 7.9 percent of the American population is now foreign born, up from 6.2 percent in 1980 and 4.7 percent in 1970. The number of foreign born residents nearly doubled in California in the past decade, to 6.5 million or 21.7 percent of the state's population.

Across the United States, the two top cities were in Florida: Hialeah City, with 70.4 percent of its 188,000 people, followed by Miami at 59.7 percent.[6]

California also ranks high among the Koreans, with roughly 144,000 in Los Angeles County. More than 25,000 of those Koreans live in the San Gabriel Valley and Whittier areas, with the largest concentrations in Diamond Bar and Rowland Heights. Jay Kim, the nation's first Korean-American, was elected to Congress in November, 1992.

If California represents the future of America, then Los Angeles may be the future of California. Already there is no racial majority in either Los Angeles city or county. All the stereotypes are obsolete. All groups include those who desire to maintain their original culture, and live as they did in the country of their birth.

In the city of Los Angeles, 3 million Hispanics constitute one-third of the city's total population, and represent the largest concentration of Latinos in the nation. Also, 35% of the nation's 7.2 million Asians live in California. Given the concrete challenges that California faces in trying to absorb so many diverse groups - challenges to the school system, the housing market, the job market, the infrastructure - it is ironic that the church can serve the better for it. It stands to win on every level of the spectrum. In the church where everyone is born into the family, and where there is neither Jew nor Greek so to speak, there is an opportunity to not only relieve the tensions that tend to bring cultural clashes, but to serve God in the process as we expend our efforts to evangelize every culture, every creature.

On the horizon, California's population grows ever more diverse. As immigration floods into formerly black neighborhoods, interracial marriages will be more acceptable, and at least in these areas the color lines will become less distinct. The new scene emerging will bring changes that will make the past seem to have been a snail pace as America's changing face rapidly accelerates.

As reported in USA Today, June 8, 1993, Chinese desperate for a new life pay up to $30,000 to escape to the United States. At those prices, smugglers are getting bolder- creating a monstrous problem for immigration officials. [7]

Recently the Immigration and Naturalization Service were challenged as a ship load of illegal Chinese immigrants were dumped ashore in San Francisco. Officials reported after the incident that they saw no end to the rising problem.

While the illegal Chinese immigration numbers are still low, INS officials predict that Chinese human rights violations will continue to result in illegal immigration. Since 1991, the INS has caught 16 ships in U. S. waters and arrested 1,700 illegal Chinese attempting to enter California. The scene then moved to New York. Those smuggled through the U.S./Mexican border are also on the rise: 500 during a recent five month period.

What is so sad is that most illegal immigrants who are captured have the same desire: to find peace and a better way of life. Yet for that opportunity, they many times commit themselves to prostitution, sweatshops, or become soldiers in gang warfare. Most who take such desperate measures are farmers trying to escape poverty and political persecution. Others are people who just want to be united with relatives already living here. In as much as illegal smuggling is one of their activities, these innocent people become victims of international crime rings.

If we were appalled at the slavery trade of early America, then we should understand that the real culprit among the recent Chinese activity are not the immigrants themselves, but cruel smugglers who cram a small rusty freighter with as many as 300 Chinese nationals. It's a modern slave trade! Each have been convinced they will find easy work and rich relatives, and pay the price. For a recent ship that ran aground off Rockaway Beach, there was approximately $9,000,000.00 involved. Smuggling human cargo is a multi-million dollar business. These people do not understand they have been exploited by gangsters known as "snake heads", until they have reached the United States and pushed off onto the shore with no where to go.

The Chinese who were apprehended in San Francisco were dirty, sick, broke, tired and disoriented. One Chinese young man spoke the sentiment of the rest as he declared, "This isn't bravery. This is for our lives." When asked about the accommodations aboard the ship, he said, "Food and water were scant: one meal a day, mostly rice, no meat, and we haven't had a shower in two months."[8]

Like California on the west coast, Miami, Florida, stands out in the east as the example of multi-racial change taking place. Like many cities where converging cultures clash, Miami's ethnic mix sometimes boils over. At any time, each of the city's racial and ethnic groups-Hispanics, Anglos, African-Americans, Haitian Blacks, and Jamaicans on a lesser degree- is primed to clash.

Some members of the other groups resent Hispanics, who began arriving in great numbers in Miami during the 1960s. Now, Hispanics are a majority, giving rise to fears among Anglos and Blacks of lost political power and job opportunities.

Due the wide cultural difference between the American Blacks and the Haitian immigrants, all the ambiguities that difference implies erupt into violent clashes. Add the Hispanic ingredient, and the area becomes explosive.

There are pockets of individuals who have been interested in bridging some of these cultural differences. But I think it is fair to say there remains a significant amount of frustration, mistrust, and to some extent, mutual hostility. Most generally from these concentrated pockets of culture, tensions must be interpreted as desperate cries for help! The church can tap into that void and bring peace to troubled hearts.

It is not the first time in history that the church was able to take advantage of social disorder. Today it has the possibility of not only serving an apparent need, but to enhance the machinery of world-evangelism in the process.

Jesus' parting instructions to his disciples on Mount Olives bring into focus every person's undeniable right to become a member of his church. He placed upon the shoulders of his followers the responsibility of reaching the entire world with the only saving gospel. He further insisted that every creature have the opportunity to make the choice to become his disciple. That choice can be made by the Hispanic, the Haitian, or the Russian.

The reason for evangelizing the world was not lost upon the church, for from the onset Jesus established the urgency: "...he that believeth and is baptized shall be saved, and he that believeth not shall be damned."

Our progress relative to this initiative while very positive, has seen a tremendous struggle between dedicated men and women with a steadfast commitment, and a staggeringly increasing world population to magnify the responsibility. However, our purpose remains constant: to present unto our Lord the church that he so unquestionably desires. A church without spot or wrinkle, but a church made up of His creatures from all over the world.

The conviction and courage of our missionary family is simply the United Pentecostal Church character in action. Their indomitable spirit has waged a great warfare. But, there is a negative in that we race the shadows of a setting sun.

While we do not wish to focus intently upon the problem, we must not ignore that woven into the fabric of the problem may very well rest the logical solution. Compare the statistics of the above chapters filled with dry facts and figures, and you come up, not with a championing of the cause of immigration, but that there is a master-plan at work in the mind of God.

The Lord of the harvest, moved with compassion to reach his world, began in these last days to bring those yet unevangelized within easy reach of the church. Every known culture has taken up residence in the neighborhoods of our North American church. Thus he provided an ingenious process in that every city has become a mission field, and every believer a missionary. This is certain to alter the process of world evangelism.

Since the only purpose for which a church exists is that it reach the community in which it has been established, it will serve a two fold purpose: 1) To reach those variegated cultures with the message of salvation, and perhaps more significantly, 2) to pour into them the urgency to reach their own kind. With this program working skillfully, instant missionaries without need of language nor cultural training will be produced.

The powerful concept is merely a simple equation. That every church have a moral obligation to reflect the racial make-up of the community it serves, and perhaps more importantly, the church represent the diversity of its community to understand, and adequately meet the needs of the people-all the people-it serves.

It would not be difficult to develop a strong relationship with representatives of the minority community, who after establishing that relationship, would be more than willing to offer suggestions, and help advance progressive evangelism strategies. Soon word would be published that interest is genuinely displayed by the church, and this would multiply the positive attitude of a good approach.

The church could then step to the front to identify people with leadership potential, and put into practice certain training programs that would duplicate the process many times over.

This one adjustment of attitude would solve the greatest question of the ages: how to reach the world of nearly 6 billion people before Jesus comes after his church. It is my opinion that he has provided the solution. It will be our responsibility to take advantage of it, and mold it into the workable plan he had in mind by making us a nation of nations.

With this thought in mind, there is no valid excuse for not evangelizing the ethnic cultures of our nation. The cause of Christ is far too important, failure too permanent, and the immigrant's need too urgent to allow our church windows to be darkened to them. Our programs should become evangelistic tools and include the total community. The United Pentecostal Church stands in a unique position to satisfy the spiritual needs of our resident guests.

Generally there are many resources from which to draw the potential membership of the local church. With a little contemplation, productive programs of evangelism can be initiated to tap into these resources. The ethnic peoples- especially those of first-generation immigration- are hungry for companionship. They are fearful and at times lost in the maze of a new culture. They search for love among the thousands of prejudice-bearing faces and feel depressed in their quest. Usually they come from homes where hospitality is a part of their nature, second only to family preservation: And they are people!

When we realize that the first-generation immigrant often cannot understand the language content of his adopted land, nor conform immediately with its culture, we should be moved to compassion instead of adopting the secular disdain. If we can dispel our fears and implement our desire to evangelize the ethnic groups- whatever the sacrifice- we will set into motion a growth that will bulge the seams of our churches.

When we work with the first-generation immigrant, using language and culture as tools of evangelism, we invest in a secure program. While working with him in the language of his birth, we are by direct association bringing his children- the second generation- into our churches. Further investment of time for indoctrination will insure our investments, and by an automatic process, the third generation will be a prominent factor within the church.

On the other hand, if we do not expend ourselves to present the gospel to the first-generation immigrant in the language of his birth, we will lose the second generation, and we will never know the third.

The subject of immigration is not new to North America, but it is demanding attention increasingly as the process of time transforms the country. Cultures from all over the world flow legally- and illegally- to assimilate into the American way of life. Our borders become horizons of hope to the world that lives beyond us. For much of the world, only an invisible line need be crossed.

We must take advantage of the many migrating people who represent all the Spanish cultures to the south, and turn frustration into productive advances for the church. If everyone will work in harmony to respect authority and incorporate the results into the body, we will see the kingdom displayed in all its glory. It is the kingdom principle we must adhere to, not personal ideology, as God moves to bring about a more productive harvest.

There are always those who have dreamed big dreams, and the longer they dream, the more powerful the dream motivates. When that dream begins to materialize, nothing can destroy the confidence in the Utopia to be apprehended. In the heart of the dreamer resides a faith that whatever the cost necessary to cross the border, it will be justified; all problems will be solved immediately upon arrival.

However, once on the north side of the border, frustration, turmoil, and fear replace the confidence that the dream had provided. The realization dawns slowly that a world of fantasy does not have the answer. Difficult times come, and the heart searches to acquire new faith. That is where the church steps in to provide answers.

Footnotes:

[1] Time Magazine - Special Issue - "The Changing Face of America."
[2] Time Magazine - Special Issue - "The Changing Face of America."
[3] San Gabriel Tribune - King Features Syndicate - Roger Hernandez
[4] U.S. Census Report For 1990
[5] The San Gabriel Tribune - L. A. Chung - June 30, 1993
[6] Based on the 1990 U.S. Census Report
[7] USA Today - June 8, 1993 - Bruce Frankel
[8] USA Today - June 8, 1993 - Bruce Frankel

Chapter Five
New Dimensions In World Evangelism

Information contained in the preceding chapters indicates that a formidable responsibility rests upon the shoulders of the church. The world- all of it- must be touched with the gospel in a seemingly impossible time frame. But, United Pentecostals as a whole are a determined, tough minded and independent people. That is why the commission to evangelize the world with the gospel became a worth while challenge. They have sent missionaries to an incredible number of countries around the world, translated the gospel message into myriads of languages and dialects, and have adapted themselves to situations unheard of to propagate their faith.

The strategies to make world evangelism effective is indicative of our leaders, and the willingness to finance missionary efforts became a characteristic of the constituency. Our people planned carefully, and executed well. The results have well proven that as an international church, we have poured the same stamina into our converts.

As a result of unending advances into the spiritual arenas of the world, a new question began to arise. What kind of effective program did the United Pentecostal Church need to realize it's global vision? Fears become evident when bottom-line results are compared to the population explosion taking place in this day. With the coming of the Lord so near at hand, will we be able to accomplish our task in time? With efforts facing a setting sun and lengthening shadows that reflect Jesus' words, "....the night cometh when no man can work....", the Lord of the harvest began moving the grain to the proximity of the barns. Representatives of every culture in the world suddenly appeared within reach of effective North American pulpits. Local neighborhood believers became missionaries, and Multicultural Ministries was given birth.

An idea that any ministry will replace our fantastic Foreign Missions policy is simply not realistic. But in as much as immigrants strive to keep their culture alive, and through dedicated continuity of indigenous language survival, certain adjustments did appear favorable. Multicultural Ministries took up the slack and provided the fellowship with the necessary securities to protect harmony in the assimilation of new converts.

There were so many factors that it would be wrong to say threats were not posed. By situational usage of ethnic personalities, and new possibilities emerging, pressures never before confronted made themselves to be felt throughout the fellowship. It had to be proven that Multicultural Ministries was not subplanting established efforts, merely enhancing them. Growth and compatibility underlined a wider spectrum of communication, language versatility met local church demands, and a reciprocal process of change enabled each local church to excel in exerting a total evangelism program.

Irrational attitudes forced a focus upon the fledgling ministry. Due this intense scrutiny, many myths were exposed. Such a one was that it would be difficult to develop a multi-cultural congregation. When the truth was revealed, it was found not to be difficult- only different.

Consciousness of political rebounds, a broad blanket of protection settled concerns and incorporated official under girding. The church began to unite behind this beautiful activity. Crossing the barriers of language and culture in a display of "For God so loved the world...." attitude, we embraced those of differing cultures, accepted their values, and defused conflicting cultural offenses with amazing success. This allowed to emerge the "first-fruits" of Multicultural Ministries. Now that the success pattern has effectively woven itself into the fabric of our church families, will we as a church continue the thrust to effectively open the door for this pioneer effort? In spite of a low financial return on investments in the implementation as we train our ethnic converts, will we think in terms of evangelism and the purpose of our existence as a church rather than an investment motive?

Due to differences in religious background training, the masses of minority language groups do not value the content of our message sufficiently to motivate their interest. It is therefore our responsibility to awaken their spiritual appetites by bringing them face to face with reading materials- in their language- and acquaint them with the gospel. When their minds are energized to accept the values of our message, we will have opened a new frontier of thought as it pertains to evangelism. As that possibility emerges- even though profit should never be equated against evangelism- even the market for training materials and other printed matter will have been created.

Training our emerging Ethnic leaders will bring forth a broad new horizon of missionary endeavors. Men and women qualified by natural birth, prepared and made capable by spiritual birth, will translate to ready made candidates for missionary service to their own cultures. World evangelism will then take on new dimensions.

Of course, multicultural evangelism will never be totally free of negative reactions, neither from those who possess that which can effectuate a powerful change in the hearts of foreign cultures, nor from those whose mind must be effected by a change of values toward Christ. Fear on both sides will be a formidable foe to conquer. But thinking in the channels of world evangelism, those negative reactions in the heart of the church will be transformed to promising possibilities of future expectation in the form of effective methods.

The name Special Ministries replaced the old term Ethnic Ministries by popular demand of our pastors, and was then later changed to Multicultural Ministries. This evangelism program of the General Home Missions Division incorporated missionary principles and methodology to penetrate minority cultures with the gospel. Targeting the congested areas of North America where the many pockets of variegated society settled, a concentrated attempt to bring them into our churches was made. While the mega-cities of our continent are similar in many ways, there is no common thread more visible than that each are home to representatives of much of the world's population. Using Los Angeles as an example, let me explain in greater detail how we have implemented Multicultural Ministries.

Los Angeles a mission field?

As new chapters are being written about the intriguing mission field on domestic soil, the one that we can now view from our back doorstep, nowhere in the world can the perspective come into focus with a more perfect contrast than in Los Angeles.

The city of Los Angeles is only one city among the many throughout North America that is going through tremendous and tumultuous change, but it will serve as a prime example of those changes taking place in Metropolitan North America. Cities in Canada such as Vancouver, Montreal, and Toronto are also feeling the effects of cultural adjustments.

First settled in 1781, Los Angeles has a rich heritage to share with the rest of the world. The two centuries it has spanned have seen the settlement develop into a great city- the second largest in North America. It is also the largest Spanish speaking city in North America, and second only to Mexico City in its population of Mexican descendency. [1]

To travel the streets of Los Angeles is to glimpse America's multicultural future. At the active playgrounds a dozen shades of kids occupy the slides, burrow through simulated tunnels and race down the catwalks, not much minding that no two of them speak the same language. Parents of grade school children say they rarely know the color of their youngster's best friends until they meet them; it never seems to occur to the children to say, since they have not yet been taught to care.

According to the Census Bureau, Los Angeles now covers a five-county sprawl bigger than Connecticut. Of its 14 million residents, 3 million arrived in the last decade from many foreign countries. Domestic born whites, who in 1960 represented 92 percent of the population, have become the minority at 49 percent. New York is the next city of diversity, followed by Miami, Florida.

Los Angeles has always been a place of change. Dramatic changes are taking place today and without doubt will be recorded in the chronicles of history. While it was founded as the "City of Angels", it is now becoming known as the "City of Immigrants." People are flooding into Los Angeles from all over the world, looking for a new home and new opportunities.

Into this complex, urban world are pouring tens of thousands of immigrants, legal and illegal (many prefer to call themselves "undocumented," seeing the problem to be more a lack of documents than a violation of law). The region is a microcosm of the population of the world. It is a city where no more than 30 percent of the population is affiliated with any kind of religious organization, and less than 20 percent attend on a regular basis. Of those who do attend, a high percentage are Roman Catholic. In downtown Los Angeles, there are more Buddhist temples than traditional Protestant Christian churches.

In addition to its white English population, the city of Los Angeles is home to 1,500,000 Mexicans, 275 thousand Spanish from South and Central America, 662 thousand Blacks, 168 thousand Germans, 80 thousand Chinese, 76 thousand Japanese, 68 thousand Filipinos, 50 thousand Koreans, 31 thousand American Indians, 31 thousand Puerto Ricans, 25 thousand Cubans, and 25 thousand Vietnamese, among other cultures.[2]

Through Multicultural Ministries the General Home Missions Division adopted a plan to reach the minority language groups in this city, and others like it in North America. The strategy of that plan was to target Los Angeles because of its distinct population complex as the place to plant a pilot program. This program was to be exported to the entire North American evangelism process.

In this limited area alone, there are more people than in 35 particular states of the United States. There are more Blacks than 7 African nations each have, more American Indians than all but one reservation in the United States, more Hispanics than 11 Latin American capitals, plus large concentrations of Filipinos, Chinese, Korean and Japanese groups. Eighty-three language groups are spoken, and in one public school alone there are 60 languages and dialects among it's student body.[3]

A simple plan was put into motion with cooperation of The Home Missions Division on both the General and District level. I, a returned Foreign Missionary from Ecuador, was to be the coordinator of this activity. Upon appointment, I outlined a strategy I felt would be productive. (1.) Awaken our pastors in the area to the potentials of cross-cultural evangelism. Then (2.) Assist local churches to establish congregations by targeting the area's minority language group, and overseeing the new workers involved; giving guidance for reaching particular segments of the multi-cultural population. The next step would (3.) Train workers with on-job training for certain language and cultural groups, and (4.) Establish a goal of establishing multi-congregations in each of our churches, urging the English congregation to mother as many of these as deemed possible.

As each pastor was educated to the importance of cultural identity among the minority groups, and the vital recognition of allowing language liberties, culture barriers began to be broken down. The church became a positive influence as new people entered from the Spanish-speaking south, and church affiliation gained a confidence. Other languages began to blend as they felt the freedoms to worship in their own language.

After 96 months of continuous and intense ministry, both in preparation and implementation of the program, 84 new Spanish congregations were given birth, with ministering activity among the Korean, Japanese, Mandarin (Chinese), Hmong, Cambodian, Lao, Samoan, Romani (Gypsy), and Tagalong (Filipino) language groups to form an additional 12 congregations.

Cross-cultural evangelism is becoming very popular among the United Pentecostal Churches of the Western District where the church is seen, not as a white or Anglo church, but as a church where two or more congregations are worshipping under a common pastor. Usually the mother church is an "English-speaking" congregation which opens its facility and government umbrella to other in-house congregations of whatever culture or language group that exists in the area.

The Unified School System uses 80 languages in their education process.[4] The church should feel if the Los Angeles school system can use over 80 languages to teach a secular education, should not our churches diversify its witness to bring the gospel in the "heart language" of such a varied population?

Many of our new converts have returned to native homelands and become a part of the church there. In some areas these returning people have established new congregations by carrying the message to the yet unreached. Some of our strongest leaders in the multicultural ministry were converted on the foreign mission field, and have brought wonderful spiritual insight to the Los Angeles endeavor.

Yes, the job is being done. Yes, we are working to improve our efficiency and modify the program until it can be exported with greater degrees of success.

That there are new challenges to be faced in the future, we do not doubt, but we feel more capable to stand up to them. The United Pentecostal Church of the Western District has had a taste of cross-culture evangelism, and I doubt seriously if any pastor who has experienced the flavor of success in this area will ever return to a single culture evangelism. They probably could not feel comfortable unless they see the variegated patchwork of color, and hear the sounds of a multilingual worship.

Other benefits have also been produced. The General Home

Missions Division has stepped to the front to lead the domestic church into revival. While World missions has reached a point where the mother church is straining to provide for anticipated growth on foreign soil, we can see where this ministry can supply a viable answer. Reaching our minority language groups will under gird the church with a more profoundly interested constituency who will reach for those of their culture, and out of whom will flow potential missionaries to assist our overburdened missionary program. We have become just people reaching people!

With startling statistics like these it is obvious we will need to have a strategy for reaching them. How would Jesus have viewed these masses if he were on earth today? I think we already know the answer to that question. He would roll up his sleeves and go into the people business.

First he would look upon them with compassion. Matthew 9:36 states, "But when he saw the multitudes, he was moved with compassion." He saw them not just as a mass but as individuals who were hurting and in need.

Thus a strategy for evangelizing is best formulated by looking at the task through the eyes of our Lord Jesus- attempting to see their needs, the opportunities, and then minister to them. If Jesus was in our world today, and faced with this challenge, He would walk the streets and the countrysides groaning with compassion.

Both national leadership and missionaries will surely need an innovative program if our church is going to impact the teeming, ever growing numbers of our day- much less the numbers of tomorrow. While the task is a formidable one, we are up to it. We readily see that for each culture, a different approach is called for. Multicultural Ministries will simply step to the pulpit and administer the gospel.

The first thing is to locate the responsive people. Some are the hidden persons that God has prepared for this particular time in history. It will be up to us to awaken their confidence that they are a part of the answer, without making them a part of the problem. Finding them is a problem.... convincing them is a problem.... and injecting them into the mainstream is a problem. After finding them we need to concentrate out energies and resources to propel them to success. At this point they become to answer.

There is near universal agreement among all of us that world evangelism is the purpose for the church's existence, and that the commission Jesus gave the disciples was to go into all the world. This means that every culture must be given an equal opportunity to experience his saving grace. What then, is the obstacle? Probably nothing more than formidable mental barriers caused by spiritual objectives weighed in secular planning actions. Perhaps the influence of cultural pride overriding the spiritual purpose we represent. Whatever the obstacle, for the benefit of the Kingdom of God, we must modify our attitude to bring it in tune with the responsibility of the church, and step into the arena to wage a successful fight.

That the results of Multicultural Ministries will be forthcoming from the church's endeavors is guaranteed, given the accounts of future constituents of heaven. John says that they will come from every nation, tongue, kindred and people. As the church recognizes this will become a reality, we are relegating all the responsibility to the hope of training men in language and culture for a mission's responsibility.

Foreign Missions has always been a positive side of the church's resources, and it will never be replaced. That is a fact well understood from the beginning. But emerging upon the horizon is that God is opening avenues for commissioning men of foreign culture to become representatives of this truth. Coming from the successful preaching of domestic pulpits, converts of a thousand cultures are burning with desire to witness to their homelands. And, since the news is getting around that it can be relatively easy to pastor a multi-lingual congregation, these successes will multiply many times over. It means that Foreign Missions will remain in its position as world-wide thrust, but that goals state-side must stimulate reforms that will reach those same cultures residing in astronomical numbers on domestic soil.

Our goals are very ambitious. For example, we were able to produce at record breaking pace, an impact that has educated local pastors that within reach of his pulpit is a multi-cultural congregation. There is a need to further educate the results in these endeavors that the doors are indeed open, notwithstanding racial undercurrents, and that every church must be free of prejudice.

Are these goals obtainable? I believe they are. We are all former aliens from the Kingdom of God. We have all obtained mercy. We are in a developing state, and reflect a gleam of God's love for his world.

Goals cannot be set, nor are they obtainable without waging a sincere effort on every level. There is no valid basis upon which we can build a case for remaining inactive relative to evangelizing our ethnic cultures, and assimilating them without fear into the machinery that reaches our world. This means that we must spearhead a drive that will involve the efforts of both constituent and the leadership of the church. We need to set our financial goals to include the proper tools of evangelism to reach the same cultures residing within the reach of home-town UPCI pulpits.

The language of Multicultural Ministries has clarity. The program has wide support. The constituency has reacted favorably. Therefore, our future initiatives should have catalytic effect. Our efforts should not be a mere timid embrace- it must be a consuming dedication. Qualified programs must be allowed to develop. What we do not need is for a secular mind to continue to control the spiritual offensive. We do not need a superior attitude that God's church should be a replica of a single culture. That truth must emanate from all quarters involved.

What about the world that is coming to us? Do we love the world any less because they rub shoulders with us in North America? Should we concentrate only on those who remain there.... so we can report progress here? Does our attitude relative to the commission change because they have migrated to our shores? The answer, of course, is a resounding no to the latter three questions if we come to a proper attitude with the former.

A number of things that have transpired during my crusade for Multicultural Ministries has given me great satisfaction, but I am the most pleased about the comfort we have accepted the One-Church concept. One for all! If the UPCI is not big enough to give equal place to all cultures in the world- in the face of Jesus' love for the world- then it is not big enough for any.

The history of the UPCI has positively embraced a love for the whole world. Missionary buzz-words include the statement, "The sun never sets on the United Pentecostal Church International." But we cannot allow ourselves the pleasure of sitting back to merely enjoy the aroma of past victories, a great majority of the world is still lost. However, we can treasure the fact that the past is in our hearts- guarded jealously- while the future yet remains in our minds. We will plan accordingly.

Despite all the advances, I am convinced we can go farther. Our goal must be to wage a continual battle to awaken our constituency to the awareness of world-evangelism. The constituency must be constantly reminded that this responsibility is not an option, but a mandate for the church. As long as one member's concern has not translated into a commitment for revival, our job is yet incomplete.

Within our fellowship the seeds of desire to reach our generation- all of it- have been planted. Dedicated cultivation has driven the people to share financial resources relentlessly until the local church wall has become a symbol of that participation. Missionary PIM pictures don the sanctuary with pride. Yet a continual appeal for further participation has elicited a cry of despair from many struggling pastors. Has the fellowship become saturated? No, I do not believe that. World evangelism is our business and we will rise to meet the challenge. While we may face the possibility to cut back on trivia, or take another look at an accepted lavish lifestyle that produces no convert for heaven, those adjustments will be made because we are the church.

Finances however, are not the resources that will ultimately perform for the United Pentecostal Church. It will be the raw materials we are mining from the many ethnic cultures residing within the productive fields of

North America. The new challenge will be to develop quality missionary personnel who will return to the countries of their origin- without the need of language training- and preach the glorious news of the kingdom.

The innovative districts across our fellowship- especially those more closely aligned to the ethnic- have begun to equate possibilities against responsibilities and are pleased with the prospects of the future. Not only has Multicultural Ministries produced strong local congregations by assimilating ethnics into the body, but has also equipped them with a strong sense of burden for family and friends residing on distant shores. Many are the missionary stories relating to families won by the testimony of a son or daughter who, having found God at a Pentecostal altar located somewhere in North America, wrote home to appeal to love ones to locate the UPCI congregation at once. These personal letters are written with such inspiration family members are mesmerized by them. The result: a new convert for the missionary church!

Bringing the focus back to North America, we are faced with the problem of getting these same people to understand that we want them to be a part of our churches in the United States and Canada as much as we want them in our churches established in their own countries- even in massive numbers!

Footnotes:

[1] Time Magazine -Special Issue "The Changing Face of America"
[2] U.S. Census Report - 1990
[3] U.S. Census Report - 1990
[4] USA Today - March 13, 1993

Chapter Six
International is a Big Word

At a relatively recent General Conference convening in Louisville, Kentucky, I was impacted by re-occurring familiarity- flags of many nations adorning the platform, exhibit areas, and projects. I joined the crowd as I erected my booth for Spanish Ministries. Displaying a decoupage map of North America, I crowned it with 22 flags to represent those Spanish cultures who reside within the United States and Canada. I was symbolizing the need for cross-cultural evangelism.

The representation of the various cultures of the world by the display of its flag to the constituency of the United Pentecostal Church must do more than awaken interest, it must move us to responsibility.

During a similar General Conference several years ago, delegates legally added the word International to the name of our organization. Those delegates gave special meaning and purpose to our constituency. Proudly, we missionaries on foreign soil at that time announced to our national churches that we were international in name as well as scope.

But internationalism is more than the display of a flag! It is a blending, an intermingling in the Body of Christ- a joining, a brotherhood. It presupposes equality. It can bear no sense of racial, cultural, or economical superiority. Internationalism is an attitude.

Every time I insert the word International after United Pentecostal Church, I feel a sense of awe. It is a big word, but more than this it has a big meaning. Even the abbreviation UPCI has greater impact than UPC. Perhaps I can pose a question for us to ponder, "Are we worthy of the addition?" Maybe better phrased is the question, "Are we truly International, or merely involved in evangelism around the world?"

Internationalism is a voluminous word. It carries a lot of content. And that, of course, makes it something of a frightening word, because we are not sure how far reaching it might be.

Three phrases have been especially associated with the word International with respect to the function of United Pentecostal Churches around the world: Self-propagating, self-governing, and self-supporting. The word International denotes that wherever there exists a United Pentecostal Church, there are certain rights and responsibilities that belong to the congregation of that church. That would be true whether the church is found in Missouri or Ecuador, in Toronto or Tanzania, in Indiana or India, Arizona or England, New York or Japan. The history of the United Pentecostal Church International around the world is impressive and we must address the need of what to do about the results.

The last decade has been a time when the word "nationalism"

weighed heavily upon the fears of the leadership. We faced the challenge and transmitted to our constituency that The United Pentecostal Church International was not simply a denomination existing world-wide, nor were we an alliance of nationally affiliated churches. We were an international fellowship of related family members, people who share in the common heritage of a great redemption, and who are giving ourselves to a great task.

We further expressed that our mission as a church was to glorify God and extend His kingdom around the world. Our objective was to spread the message of salvation wherever the need exists, and wherever possible plant another church of like precious faith. This we testified by adding the word International to our name.

The impact of this will carry a lot of influence upon the fulfillment of the church's responsibility. Contrary to this, if the First World church because of its giving expects that the Third World church become its subjects, then an attitude of ownership is insinuated. However, since the head of the church is Christ, the word International merely conveys that rights and responsibilities will be shared equally, as well as relationship in the fellowship.

The ministerial delegation of the fellowship answered both a no and a yes respectively to these questions. Yes, the First World church will share authority as one of its responsibilities, and the Third World church will share responsibility as well as rights. Rights and responsibilities cannot be separated. Self-propagation, self-government, and self-support are sacred privileges for United Pentecostals everywhere and anywhere, and as we applied the word International to our name, we intended that a distinct message be conveyed to the world.

In the understanding of this change there came also the acknowledgment that no difference will be made in the United Pentecostal who cannot speak English, and the United Pentecostal who cannot speak Spanish. We view all the body as our family, and in the context of each of their own respective responsibilities and opportunities there is an expectation of sharing in the results.

Internationalism also dims the spotlight in specific areas where it has been the strongest. It will not focus attention or emphasis on any one world culture. Eastern or Western, First World or Third World.

Internationalism means that the whole world is His creation without favoritism toward any, and that He alone is the ultimate answer for any continent, or race of people.

If we consider the word International properly, it moves us away from focus on how we differ and draws attention to that which we have in common: a ministry to a broken and hurting world. It moves us away from an "us- them" mentality in reference to our church's operation. We think less in terms of "foreign missions" and "home missions", and more in terms of world missions- at my doorstep or around the world.

The impact of the word International results in a removal of all language and cultural barriers in the church, paving the road to a one-church concept. It will be that church that will step to the throne and put on the display of splendor as is recorded in Revelations 13. The preview of that church is demonstrated in the church who says, "We are His family, on His mission, to His world."[1]

Footnotes:

[1] Nazarene Monthly

Chapter Seven
Strategies That Serve Our Best Interests

Logic tells us that unless we are guided by a clear strategy, world evangelism cannot be realized. Yet would Jesus, whose mission to the world initiated the task, have issued such a commission to the church had it not been possible? I am convinced that world evangelism is not only possible, but within our grasp if we can develop the strategy for its success.

A strategy sets priorities that serve prominent interests. Therefore as a church, we must seek out strategies that best serve those interests, and which ones serve poorly, or not at all. The very reason for the United Pentecostal Church International to exist is for the propagation of the gospel. A vision of a lost world around us, and the regions beyond, has produced a sensitivity in the church to achieve all that evangelism implies. Whatever else our sensitivity has shown, it has demonstrated that we have developed a machine that can perform the task, if allowed to function in areas that can project the deciding strategy for this decade.

While many evangelism thrusts of the past have been reduced to guarding the constituency on the periphery, we must somehow modify the program to focus on major offensives that will multiply our successes.

There has never been an era of time since Christ that such extensive and diverse series of events, activities, and litanies been utilized to propel evangelism as has our modern day. By the same measure it can be said that neither has any era produced such a fervor of excitement and enthusiasm for world evangelism- a fact that is proven by multi-million dollar investments to perform it- as has today's Body of Christ.

While the United Pentecostal Church International has a lot to do to make world evangelism meaningful enough to succeed, it has indeed been about the Father's business. To be effectively successful however, the fulfillment of Jesus' commission, so eloquently etched in the hearts and minds of millions by his emotional appeal on Mount Olives, must become the all consuming mandate of today.

Todaywe see real possibilities along with challenges. Those possibilities and challenges warrant candor about where we actually stand, particularly for those in position of leadership. Not our preaching sermon, nor our biblical platform, but our practicing sermon. That which we do and think when there is no congregation to observe.

An up todate exposure of our purpose will suffice. Was it a reasonable proposal to reach into every nation and make disciples? Does this strategy still provide for the church the viable program to evangelize the entire world? Was not Christ's purpose in using this strategy to plant in each nation witnesses to spread the gospel to that nation? Was this strategy more plausible in the days of Christ when cultural walls stagnated attempts to reach the regions beyond? Or today when the world is at our fingertips, accessible by both education and understanding of cultural values, while world travel has been made easier by transportational ingenuity. It seems that the reasons for not having accomplished world evangelism has each taken on a life of its own. End results has had innuendo and suspicion smothering the life of each forward step that might have provided a successful strategy.

Who benefits most when challenges remain unmet? Why? Should not we then accept changes that will both safe-guard results, and send invading forces with a clear strategy that will add to our success patterns? Is it possible that human nature among us dictates that personal glory must have substance before challenges are met with vigor and constancy of purpose? Further, is it possible that those most involved feel so sensitive about the controls of decisive strategy until rational debate can not begin to address the initiative with clarity?

We have come to the point when our fellowship has the right to view itself, and have others view it, as one of the main proponents for world-evangelism. We should not be faced with a need to compete with evangelism stereotypes whose covert purpose is to propagate personal interests worldwide. A candid investigation into our message should develop confidence in the motives of our leaders and with that confidence allow a successful strategy emerge out of their constructive view. It is time that priority rule out personal interests, and challenges to initiatives be viewed as a sharpening of the sickle rather than an attack upon character or ability.

Our vast national resource of multicultural population then becomes another issue of concern. While it appears a separate problem for the local church, could it be possible that in determining strategy for evangelism, we have discovered a far more valuable resource than finances? Spiritual justice should be at the heart of discussion as we plan strategy touching world-evangelism. Can there be successful strategy without the participation and the involvement of those who are directly affected by our planning? Why isn't it possible to view a conquest attack upon world evangelism by enlisting those most capable of succeeding? Do we fear the incorporation of our successes into the mechanism? Does it go beyond our perception of reality? Are we fearful of addressing a plan that may show clear results if personalities important to the planning are directly involved? Why not see the church as the early church saw it, where there is neither Jew nor Greek, bond or free, and focus upon the commission rather than the committed. Or send as he did when He spoke to the results of His evangelism, "Go home to thy friends, and tell them...." Would this strategy work well for us?

I am firmly convinced we can accomplish world evangelism in this decade by broadening the circle of involvement, training the results of evangelism, and sharing with them the glory. The spiritual arena needs more hard heads with tender hearts that are based upon changing priorities in strategy, rather than guarding a maintenance program that stifles us to a status quo. We must not compromise those who are most deserving, and the most neglected. Reaching our multicultural population must become a priority on the world-evangelism agenda.

Finally the matter of spiritual education for the development of men for ministry must become a source of constant concern. Not for the goal of mere performance on the platform of the local church, but the longer view of illuminating each his corner of the world for final conquest as it relates to world evangelism.

Educating our ministers- both among the ethnic and the home born- must move us to concern. There are simply too many functional illiterates in the ministry who have alienated more converts than they have established. This problem has reached crisis proportions, and substantially contributes to a decrease in numbers because of a high dropout rate. The gospel is more than cultural preservation or personal value contests. It is a lost world trying to find God through a maize designed to eliminate more souls than it preserves. We must attempt to deal with events that have made our age the most turbulent period in human history. I do not believe that these bewildering happenings of our day are merely the jumble of events without meaning; they are rather the media through which God is trying to break through with a clear voice about his ultimate plan in world evangelism. The real objective is that God is bringing the harvest to the barns.

Please take the time to at least study the panorama of the UPCI world-wide activity, ask yourself a few simple questions, and honestly decide where we are in the picture. Is God opening doors that will place a comma at the end of the Book of Acts and continue the history? Has He indeed designed the UPCI as a central player in world evangelism? Will we be able to evangelize the 6 billion people of the world before Jesus returns?

I would like to project some answers. Yes, God is moving the church into a new strategy to compete in the world evangelism arena. No, with the world population growth rate, and our bottom line conversion figures at present, we will not be able to fulfill the great commission in time for the rapture.

However, the Bible gives us Christ's simple evangelism principle. Try as we might, we cannot improve upon this principle, and if we will incorporate this simple strategy into our evangelism program, we CAN indeed reach the world in time. And, the good news is, we can do it with less money, and a greater chain reaction of results. We need only to re-focus on evangelism with what God is doing today in North America. The continent is host to every known culture in the world! Would you like to see this immigration problem turned around to become the world-evangelism answer? I will simplify this quickly...

In every exploding revival that spread quickly through cities and towns of the early church, there was a spark created from a casual Ethnic encounter. Let's take a more intense scrutiny at some well known biblical passages, and compare these events as an intentional pattern.

When you see Jesus talking with the woman at Jacob's well, and you focus intently, the scene holds more than meets the eye. Here you have the whole world evangelism picture in a single passage. You see the problem, but also realize that the answer is uniquely woven into the fabric of that problem. Jesus is teaching us how to evangelize our world.

This story, as you know, is a case against the background of a bitter, age long religious feud. The Jews had no dealings with the Samaritans. Josephus, the Jewish historian, described the background quite frankly. He said that when the Northern Jew wanted to go to Jerusalem he always made a detour around Samaria, which lay directly between Galilee on the north and Judea on the south. The Jew was not interested in the shortest route between the two points. He crossed the river on the north into Perea, made the journey on good Jewish territory, then recrossed the Jordan and traveled the hills into Jerusalem. He simply would not go through Samaria.

John's Gospel tells us that Jesus must go through Samaria. He, being what he was, could not detour. He could not walk a trail that prejudice had blazed. He could not perpetuate a problem that had been created by man's sin and narrowness and resentment. He had to go through it- and thereupon hangs the story in which the whole world picture can be seen at a single glance.

On the journey Jesus had a conversation with a woman, something which dismayed the disciples. Tradition was against it, custom was against it, and religion was against it. Besides, the woman was a Samaritan- and a sinner. Such a thing simply was not done! But, however wrong it seemed from the standpoint of the past, everything was right about it in the light of the dawning future.

Jesus is always out in front of us. Wherever you touch him, he is the living Herald of the dawn. He shocks us by doing things differently than we do. "Behold I will do a new thing...." God reminds us. This plan of action must be put into effect if the church is to fulfill the commission and have an acceptable ending.

First, we too must go through Samaria. Because we are Christians, because we are the church, we must route our path through modern Samaria and lead the way in breaking down the old racial barriers that impede positive world evangelism. Whatever evasion others may make, whatever detours others may want to perpetuate, we who are Christians cannot go around the problem. We must go through it, for this is the hinge upon which the doors of the next decade will swing.

If we are to write another chapter for history we must understand that the world is not our's alone. While the white, English race became an outstanding people in technology and dynamics, and through these achievements acquired a good deal of the world's real estate, he acquired much of it by conquest. At any rate he got it, and he believed it was his divine right to lord over those he considered as lesser achievers. He developed amazing skills, and had a genius for organization and industry. It was to him mostly that the light of science came. And so, without intending it or without even knowing it, the white man became the strong man, the teacher of the world. However, one of his greatest strengths has become his weakness. He understands from whence his position has come and he knows that he has not always been right, no matter how successful. In this he becomes vulnerable to prejudice, an emotion that is intended to persuade himself that he is indeed better than others.

The moral fibers of righteousness can be a protection against wrong doing. There is no refuge against wrong if intentional motives have dictated actions. There is nothing left but for common sense to correct direction, and here the cross-roads leads to confessions. Right thinking will prevail! No man can afford prejudice. It is immoral! If we continue in our condescending attitude toward those of other cultures, a pent-up resentment will explode. God never made any race to dominate over another. God made all men in his image. That is the Christian message and that is our faith. If we build on it we would send a thrill through all Samaria.

Today, as never before, we have an opportunity to go through Samaria. Notwithstanding enormous difficulties we can proceed quickly to expose Christian principles, and the whole world would rise to call us blessed.

Let us go on a bit farther. Jesus and his encounter with the woman is another matter that confronts the Christian conscience. Follow Jesus down that dusty road in Samaria to Jacob's old well under the shade trees and find another compulsion in his heart which must also be in our's. There came along a woman of Samaria to get water- not much of a person, not a college professor, neither a prince or a ruler. She was a nobody, a rather hopeless woman with her head down and her life tangled. Wouldn't you like to have heard him talk to her? He startled her because such a thing wasn't done- a man talking to a woman in public. It was against the rules of etiquette and religion then, and it still is.

Wouldn't you have liked to have heard him say, "Would you give me a drink?"- then the conversation. What makes the difference between Christ and all others is his unprecedented respect for the inherent dignity of a person- any person. Jesus never talked down to anyone. He treated every person as a great creature and always counted on something in people, even the lowliest, to respond to the highest truth. Jesus believed in people, and they believed in him because he believed in them.

On every page of the scriptures you can see him opening the door of hope to them, making them aware of what was in them, seeing the possibilities behind their appearances, and unfolding their capacities. The common people heard him gladly because to him they were not common. They carried in their souls the mark of divine image.

Jesus kindled a spark in the woman's heart- a heart in which all the lights had gone out- and that spark went like a fire throughout the community. The woman left her waterpot, and went into the city, and said... "Come see a man.... is not this the Christ?" What began as a conversation ended in a spiritual awakening of a village... a city... a people. This is why this story holds you, fascinates you- there is a hint in it of what might happen to the human spirit today with the touch of Christ upon it. We have gone as far as we can with materialism, with our own ingenuity and vision, and all the wells are empty. The churches while totally committed to the missionary cause, feel inundated with the rising financial needs to operate the machinery.

Do you see the water pitcher resting on the well side? That forgotten water jar? Mute but eloquent symbol it is of what can happen when this simple principle of evangelism goes into effect. Reach an Ethnic person with this message, and he will run with it to his community. That forgotten water pitcher stands for old things left behind after Christ has come. Old priorities, previous personal dreams for the future, old fears and shadows find a transformation taking place in the thrill of a great awakening. Soon you can hear the thunder of marching feet along the road-people coming to see the Man who sets life free.

If you take that principle, link it to Mark chapter five, and match the fabric to that of the demoniac, you have a pattern. Go home to your family, to your friends, to those to whom you can communicate with the greatest ability, and tell them what great things the Lord has done in your life. The family hears, the friends believe, and great joy results. Yes, there is indeed a pattern.

The pattern continued through the Book of Acts to give the early church the successes we read about. It is history of Jesus reaching out to lost humanity-even those across the fences of culture and language-through the results of His ministry. He utilized converts for His purpose of serving their world. Herein is contained a viable program; a strategy that will reach the entire world with this gospel before Jesus comes.

We have our work cut out for us, and there is plenty of it. However,

I believe we are closer today than we have ever been to our goals. I believe the decade of the 1990s will require and receive increased integrity, ingenuity and tenacity. We will provide it because we are the church.

Chapter Eight
Calculated Changes

In our struggles to produce a church in the world, there are forces that rise to frustrate the cause. Not the least of these struggles is the balance of equality in a "One Church" concept. Culture and language ambiguities, while a formidable ingredient to bring into focus, is not the most difficult to balance, rather it is the rapid series of changes that tend to confuse the leadership.

In order to bring responsibility into sharp focus, we who are the catalyst for change, must think strategically, and become knowledgeable of what effect changes will have on long-term goals. It is also extremely necessary to perceive how changes will relate to one another. Once cause and effect is understood, it will be possible to guide the processes flawlessly without creating unrelated trends that might tend to trigger conflict. The least favorable direction for all concerned is a collision course.

A positive, consistent pattern with distinctive goals woven into purpose, patiently building upon achievement, is perhaps the greater discernible factor that will shape the future. When progress calls for change, the indistinct factors must be carefully eliminated, and articulated projection submitted to those of the leadership for approval.

The future must be the patient, combined work of all sides of the coin, not just one. While the least favored component essential to success, time is of the greatest significance. History inundates us as to the consequences of rapid and thoughtless change. Almost invariably changes that are too rapid result in disorientation and incapacitation among those for whom change will benefit. Our principle goal is to affect the organization with controlled changes that will not overload leadership circuits. Subsequently, we will see intensified visibility for multicultural brethren that are qualified by character and capability, and this will go far to shape the mind-set of the constituency.

By calculated advances of controlled change, there is a strong reason to believe that pressures that are applied will propel us forward rather than create a confusion that could lead to a fractured relationship. Further, responsive decisions will create the atmosphere of approval where a wide dimension of indigenous mentality can produce a natural response, not only on the part of those benefiting from change, but those from whom change tends to exact sacrifice. Relative to the church, it is ironic that the very world we are endeavoring to reach with a gospel of love, runs counter to developments that would blend the results into one body.

Through interrelation of power resources we will see a change that over a period of time will have produced the greater result. A higher visibility of our multicultural brethren in national scale activity by mutual choice, will communicate good will where culture and language will not be questioned. In other words, merit will guide us to unprecedented levels. By contrast, power struggles, no matter how right the cause, will serve only to frustrate. If motive is analyzed, and crystal reason defines direction, it will elicit an appreciation on the part of those responsible for setting controls. Sometimes the trust we place in other people is based on very little more than one's measure of a man.

Successes will demand a mentality on all sides that does not think in terms of culture, but upon a criteria of scriptural qualification that will place "in the Body as it hath pleased Him." Therefore, it is not entirely incidental that our officials are opening doors to new and exciting frontiers. The timing is right, the cause is just, and the results rewarding, to bring to the door of the future a physical church that displays the attributes of the spiritual. For no where is the love of God more evident and his purpose more clear than where all the cultures of His world are worshipping together. Of course that also means that there will be chosen from "....among you... men of honest report, full of the Holy Ghost....", whom God can put over the church's business. I believe this course of action- as in the biblical account- will please all the people.

The growing volatility of racial tensions in the secular world, dramatized by power struggles intended to overwhelm, need not figure within the walls of the church. This is a foreign element that need not be utilized. A step by step purposeful removal of barriers will create trust and a blending of our peoples without consideration for color or culture. At that point we will become the church, and make obsolete any mention or thought of the origin of its constituents.

Against this background of unity, world evangelism will precede full throttle without fear of localized crises. The answer is, this blending must be accomplished without the sacrifice of those cultural values not clashing with biblical principle. It must result from every quarter and extend to the most extreme areas of cultural processes. The methodology we incorporate into strategy must be void of prejudice. We must step to the stage as men born for such an hour as this, and take the initiative into hands pure of motive apart from that which would extend the Kingdom of God.

The objective appears to be a common goal for all of us. The church in its quest to evangelize the world desires to adjust mentality to enhance its abilities. The distinctive cultures for whom evangelism is extending invitation, should by all means, strive to become an effective part of the family. All together must make sacrifices that will surrender personal ideas and principles in order to embrace the higher set of values that merge with the eternal.

The personnel who labor in harmony with the elected leadership must understand that to an established administration, changes are frightening. To step from strategies that have been successful for decades and approve of programs that are totally foreign to that which the church has practiced previously, is a responsibility demanding caution. On the other hand, caution must be merely a time to weigh the positives against the negatives, and make decisions that will favor the opportunities.

The constant need for adjustments in our evangelism strategy is dictated by the consistently changing world around us. The world we are reaching for today is nothing like the world even our past generation planned for. Even though I have written much about this subject, I'm not sure what meaning these adjustments hold for us. At the same time I firmly believe that by fine-tuning our objectives, we will see world evangelism take on a new garment. I also know that adjusting strategy is one of the most important efforts we will by necessity place high on the priority list. There is a lot of ambivalence in our projections to reach the world while we manifest a reluctance to evangelize those same cultures in the local community. Almost always, this reluctance is based upon cultural censure.

The future of the UPCI will boil down to its history- or will it? Unless we make needed adjustments, and that voluntarily, emerging situations will shape us by our inaction. It is a sad, strange state of affairs when the love of God is so impelled by the negative issues raised by secular values. All over the world men are pleading for brotherhood and peace.... Impotence results! Perhaps that is the big question we are addressing right now. Whether we will admit that we have a responsibility to change, or even admitting the need to change, we have the courage to do so. In light of "the whole gospel to the whole world," is there not a valid commitment to remove local racial barriers, and thereby broaden our capabilities on the global scale?

There is a desire to sometimes vaguely articulate in order to avoid past attitudes. We do wish to be faithful to our commission, and this brings a deeply ingrained truth to the surface that will not dissipate with the mere winds of caution. Assimilating multi-cultural results into the local church will present problems because we are dealing with people's cultural values. But if people cannot grasp the one church concept and blend into a local congregation, how can one expect to cope with it on an eternal scale.

I try to formulate the fear that the twilight of evening time will cut short any long-term options we ambiguously push forward to ease a troubled conscience. Procrastination is working over-time if we base our hope upon sufficient time syndromes.

As we edge toward the coming of the Lord, we're more aware than ever before of our power to reach the world. The first thing that strikes me with irony is how little there is to change but our attitude. An attitude change will make a major difference. A successful program of world evangelism will have to do with the way the church perceives culture. It has nothing to do with a dominant culture, but has a whole lot to do with how we view ordinary people located within our evangelism responsibility. It also has much to do with how we assimilate new converts into the spiritual family. And, a lot to do with how much cultural custom we weave into a word called godliness.

Financing world-evangelism is an important factor, but finances are powerless unless people desire to be saved. There is no doubt that our people have accepted the challenges that relate to financing our endeavors world-wide. However, with distinctive cultures pouring into our local churches in North America as a result of Multicultural Ministries, it is possible that we have discovered a far more effective resource- efficient personnel! With a change of attitude we could employ methodology that could transform our image worldwide.

The successes gained through a new attitude toward culture will be enhanced by a total confidence in the message we represent. We must make commitments to something far greater than ourselves.

In the meaningless debates about culture as it relates to the church, the central issue usually boils down to trivia. The scripture gives us a terminology more likely defined as a fusion into one body, a body in which there is neither Jew nor Greek, bond or free- one people, one church! The major theoretical result of a dominant culture mentality usually develops in fragmentation of the body. A trend of this nature, if not adjusted, debilitates the church to an ineffective dream. While the United Pentecostal Church has had several years of incremental movement forward relative to the composite of its membership, there are times when the pendulum threatens to swing in reverse direction due a revival of racial rhetoric.

This is all the more true as issues such as position and personal benefit- rather than a kingdom principle- tend to motivate key figures. It is my opinion that fine-tuning the goals from time to time to address concerns will serve to keep the focus upon the spiritual arena.

We need to maximize productivity in the body by extending participation to an ever increasing circle, incorporating multiplicity rather than an exclusive mentality. This generates a growing fraternity that will reproduce itself. There is no room in the program for attitudes such as, "...what's in it for me?" or "... what will it do for my kind?" In this type of environment, the evolving nature would prove to be detrimental to a healthy future. While we cannot be innovators and be afraid of change, we must all operate within a prescribed set of guidelines that will produce a God-ordained result.

Changes brought about by accommodating the multiplicity of personalities and styles, providing each is governed by godly principles, will give us a future that will be acceptable. Attitude is a small thing, but it makes a big difference. As a vessel, each of us must bear the marks of pressure in order that the minute design of the potter emerge in the finished product. The most common adjustment made by the potter is to fine-tune an attitude that recognizes the whole world as God's creation- equal in His sight- rather than a small segment of it. In this manner, the church can get down to business to do what it does best; evangelize the lost.

We must have an unerring instinct for the important, guided by an ability to judge which issues are peripheral and which are worthy of perseverance. In all our debate, the big picture must remain in focus. We must build consensus rather than eliminate opponents. A question, "What does God value in this situation?" is always in order. It is a chaotic world we survive in, but one that's also filled with opportunities. The important thing is to judge the difference.

We must be attracted to service as a means of doing good and measured in terms of practical results. We must never be reduced to impotence or inability. Personal benefit is a dead-end that reflects an ill choice.

Dealing with important issues to stabilize attitude on the short-term, with the goal to assimilate into the body on the long-term, is the better goal. Though time may be involved, the infrastructure of administration must be constructed with care, instead of accepting the dramatic short-term gains so alluring to a shortsighted mentality. In doing this, we will not find it necessary to constantly return to adjust attitude or direction.

With changes that bring all believers into one body, many alert pastors have viewed the massive numbers of immigrants coming into the United States as a rich harvest field, and modified their evangelism strategy accordingly. They have been rewarded handsomely as this beautiful people responded to become an integrate part of their churches.

Christians do not look upon the world as do the non-Christian, for God does not view the world as a complex conglomerate of cultures and languages. He sees the world only as His creation, and His people mirror that attitude. People are individuals, and individuals represent souls; souls for whom God has provided His church in His world.

Perhaps one of the most important things the United Pentecostal Church provides for people of any culture is a sense of belonging. More than just a church, it is a family of believers- a place where people feel the satisfaction of being a vibrant part. Our ethnic communities have found that threads of love- defying every barrier of culture- are woven into the fabric of the church's membership.

Though challenged in this day by an increasingly variegated culture where seeds of prejudice generally bias the population, the church has developed outstanding congregations that blend in harmonious relationship. All of this is being done while retaining the dignity of language and custom. Fine-tuning the program to provide an even more successful cross-culture evangelism within our fellowship has been our commitment. Because changes were implemented with care, we have not only been able to retain our ethnic sons in the gospel, but we were also able to broaden the scope of the United Pentecostal Church International.

With Multicultural Ministries presenting new horizons for the local church, we can insure a great future of continual revival and growth. However, it will be the brave-hearted who will forge ahead to blaze the trails, knowing that the masses will follow.

Whatever route we take to reach our multicultural community, we are insured of a positive destination. The biblical principle and example was established by our Lord Himself, who initiated cross-cultural evangelism to extend His kingdom. The woman at the well of Samaria; the demoniac of Gadara; the woman of Canaan who sought help for her daughter. In each situation, Jesus honored their desire for a relationship.

Chapter Nine
Surrendering Our Prejudice

This is a subject that is not going to interest a great many people. It should. The bottom line in our very purpose for existing as a church is to evangelize the world. Not just our kind, but every creature.

Relative to Multicultural Ministries, we effectuated change in the United Pentecostal Church, and we got it! Our leaders joined with us to assist in adjusting the mechanism of administration. Not that policies were replaced, but that the mentality toward the way we've always done things has been adjusted. Now with this change comes a renewed quest for world evangelism. There is no doubt new optimism is in the air; an enthusiasm that will enhance cause and effect. World evangelism is the fuel that energizes the thought pattern of the United Pentecostal Church International, and gives that particular reason in our very purpose for existing.

Evangelism among our multicultural population on the domestic front has taken on new dimensions. The rewards are tremendously positive, and the United Pentecostal Church International is surging forward with innovative programs that are reproducing our effectiveness. As a church, the cultural walls that separate us are crumbling. If anything is clear from these results, it is that we have followed the principles of Jesus' ministry of evangelism. He too, extended his ministry to other cultures, and sent the converts to bear the good news to their own kind. Of course, that is our objective! But to achieve it, there is work to be done- plenty enough to go around. We have reason to believe things can continue to change, but our optimism isn't a naive optimism of inexperience and it isn't so much a "can do", as "gotta do". The mandate of the commission requires world evangelism as a contingency to his 2nd coming! He was emphatic in that "this gospel of the kingdom shall be preached in all the world for a witness unto all nations; and then shall the end come."

The big question is, now that we have begun to produce the goals we set out to achieve, are we going to close our eyes and merely hope for the best, or are we going to get down in the trenches and perform?

Change isn't something we can leave only to the Black, the Spanish, Asians, the Russians, or any one else at our door step, it is also the responsibility of the dominant culture. Forging the new spiritual community is the work of the total constituency! Convincing the church is a job that must be taken seriously, and quickly! After successes in that arena, evangelism can then step to the cutting edge of effectiveness with results responding to a personal call to service. They (new converts) will "...preach(ed) everywhere, the Lord working with them...." In this manner, evangelism will be effectuated.

On the domestic front the transformation has been quick. No stone has been left unturned that would provide for the infusion of other cultures into the church, and that without comprising principles of language or custom brought into harmony with the scriptures. As more and more cultural groups are introduced into the North American church through the efforts of our Multicultural Ministries, we are finding ways to deal with cultural differences. We are learning that our love for God is the common factor that fuses all of us into a unified body.

Situations that magnify difference will become increasingly less difficult as the American church becomes more culturally diversified. That diversification promises to be breath taking! As a person, we may resist diverse culture acceptance, but as a church, biblical principle mandates that the whole world will be molded into one harmonious unit.

The fastest growing method that we can use to deal with ensuing problems, is a cultural awareness program which teaches our people how to value the differences that exist in the people we worship with. As the ability to motivate and work with culturally diverse groups increases, the results will translate to policy.

If one were to focus on the negative, it would be seen that most people of any culture in the world- when faced with culture difference- are too long, too often, and by too many, viewed as inferior, ignorant or lazy, and not really worthy of a realistic program of evangelism. All of us as a culture, tend to place other individuals into categories of these stereotypes. However, as a church we must realize the cross-section of any culture will show the same characteristics, given the opportunity.

The longer we delay in destroying myths that more often than not are non-existent, and break the habit of stereotyping anything that differs in cultural value, the more deeply prejudice will penetrate the self-consciousness, thereby automatically reacting when confronted with cultural decisions.

In the United Pentecostal Church International, we must begin quickly the process of breaking down cultural barriers, and that in all arenas. We must immediately shatter the common American vice of making reference to cultural jokes, and responding to humor that perpetuates the subconscious mind-set that differences in culture are equivalent to inferiority. That advice is good for any culture.

Of course, ironing out the cultural wrinkles in the church can be complicated. In the church people tend to be close and personal. Sometimes that can lead to face to face liberties that can be destructive.

Because we are possessors of the only saving gospel, and because we are an international church, we must realize that we have the responsibility of stepping into the spiritual leadership role to immediately disengage the mental tendency to automatically label people because of ethnic, language, or color difference.

To help with these adjustments of attitude, cultural diversity seminars and workshops could be taught on all levels. Education would reveal that our love for God must transcend carnal mind-set, and accept others as individuals on equal levels, rather than dropping them into stereotype categories. It's a delicate problem to approach- as people on all sides often become defensive. But workshops and technique training would assist us to face these problems, and thereby defuse subconscious reactions.

The United Pentecostal Church International is standing in the open door to end-time revival. The dream is touching our fingertips! If we will bring the love for the mission fields of the world to the correct playing field, and create viable programs for evangelism among those same cultures living in our neighborhoods, a powerful resource more adequate than finances will go to work for us.

Is it all right culturally to finance with sacrificial measure a revival on a remote mission field, rejoice over the results, and not engage ourselves to reach those same peoples residing here in the United States and Canada? Do we feel that it is best to retain the results of this revival among the culturally different at a distance? It's an interesting question to ask ourselves.

Another way to advance the positive future of cultural acceptance is to give high-visibility to those who have the capability, regardless of color, culture, or any other differing characteristic.

Smoothing out cultural differences in the church demands more than a casual approach, or even attending or teaching a seminar workshop on the subject. To make these changes real and lasting, we must set rigid goals to destroy discrimination within the body of Christ. We will know when we have arrived! It will be when any participant steps to a place of active service- be it to bestow honor or acknowledging an accomplishment, or a position of responsibility in leadership- and we accept that individual first and foremost because of his ability and not because of similar cultural values; when we have no subconscious reaction due visible difference such as color, or language. When a man's capability and ministry will provide adequate access to leadership in our congregations, districts, or among international official status, without taking into account consciously- or unconsciously- his culture or color.

Probably the most important factor for change among us is an unequivocal commitment from every level of the church that each of us will transform the secular mindset into the principles set forth by Jesus in the parable of the "Good Samaritan", that we will serve the needs of the people, and request those who sit in the shadows of our influence to "go and do thou likewise."

We will then give the present world surrounding our local churches a preview of the church in heaven: distinctive representatives of every nation, people and tongues, dancing around our altars. It boils down to a case of simply surrendering our prejudices dealing with cultural differences, and forging a new mind-set of morality and what is right. If we cannot do this we have problems too deep for simple communication to solve.

Many demonstrate another improper attitude toward people. They feel that there are so many people around that due to the responsibility relative to the great commission weighing so heavily, they would rather ignore them. The numbers are absolutely suffocating! But they can't!

In a few years, the world's population will top 8.3 billion. What makes this so important to the church is the fact that world population is our business. Our commitment to the gospel is that we will announce its good news to every creature. The time element involved indicates increasing responsibility as world population increases.

In 1850, world population stood at 1.25 billion. It was necessary for a century to pass before that figure was doubled to 2.5 billion. More importantly, within 38 years- bringing us to 1988- world population doubled again. And, say the demographers, by 2025 the 8.3 figure will have been reached. Of this figure, 7 billion will live in the third world. Economic sense tells us that the society into which they will be born can ill support them. They will first move into the already existing mega-cities, and later migrate into the First-world.

Therefore, the Christian church has a choice. It can admit the problem is too awesome, too difficult, too costly, or it can evangelize.
This is not merely a verbal expression to work up people's emotion. It means that the church will move out into the streets and aggressively present the message that will meet the need of mankind. Of course this will also mean opposing popular opinion, countering culture prejudice, facing difficult struggles, and take risks. It also means we will step outside the stained glass atmosphere of our churches and into the trenches of the real world to perform our task.

Facts of this kind are not fun to write. Hopefully it will not be fun to read. But then, neither have the facts that have impacted the secular world caused many smiles. Seemingly somebody has to die that others may live. Somebody must sacrifice that others may have, and somebody must brave the uncharted paths that others may know the way.

Christ did not call us to have fun or to be comfortable. He called us to evangelize the world. The world means people- all kinds of people- even those of other cultures. Sometimes they live across the street.

Over the years reports from the mission fields of the world have afforded an opportunity for the members of the United Pentecostal Church

International to feel the pulse of the great commission. The constituency was challenged to multi-million dollar investments. Men were moved to become involved to the extent they learned new languages, and became absorbed in new cultures. I was one of them. That will perhaps never change. However, a new chapter is being written about an equally intriguing mission field. This is the one that we can now view from the back door step of our local church.

The General Home Mission Division pauses with pen in hand, tense and trembling, yet anxious to translate energies to successes. The masses of increasing global population are seen by a church that is ready to become even more impacted with the responsibility of the great commission. A new realization has dawned that while the Foreign Missions program will always be necessary, we have at hand the same cultures who have immigrated to the local scene. Loud and clear came the directive, "We must provide a viable program of evangelism to each of these cultures in the language of their birth, and that here on the home-front".

In the secular sense, immigrants do, of course, bring a definite responsibility to a society. New customs that are unfamiliar to the host culture, a differing of needs that often upset the normal pattern of every day simplicity, new tastes, colors, and life to a community. Things previously easily understood now oft times become lost in ambiguity. But even here opportunity is tightly woven into the problem. An innovative church can provide language studies for those individuals needing instruction in English. This will serve two purposes: 1) an assistance to the community, and 2) a ministry for someone in the church searching for a place to minister.

Along with language and culture come problems dealing with personal involvement on the spiritual stage. Not only is the local scene facing a transformation, but the dynamics for world evangelism is changing as a result. Immigration opens new channels of exposure for the gospel, and when the gospel has completed its work, it will provide the world with quality witnesses for those who have never heard in depth of Jesus Christ.

Task force activity transmitted the fact that the church must take a second look at itself and clearly define, or perhaps redefine, its purpose. We have come to the point where the United Pentecostal Church International has the right to view itself, and have others view it, as the mechanism to evangelize the world. If it cannot, then we have become a club of professional ministers managing a profitable business.

The first thing realized was that the domestic church was offering the gospel of Jesus Christ only in the English language, even though in many of our prominent cities a good percentage of the population did not speak English. A plan was implemented to do something about this, and "cross-culture" evangelism was brought to birth.

One-third of North America's United Pentecostals live in multi-cultural neighborhoods, and this makes it easy to comprehend the need for change.

Indicative to a growing number of cities of North America, in the Los Angeles county school system, over 80 languages are spoken among the students. At a recent parent's night at Hollywood High School, a brief presentation by the principal took 25 minutes. It had to be translated from English to Spanish to Korean to Armenian. In some other areas the language grouping may differ, but the principles remain intact.

Uptown Argyle Street in Chicago looks like prewar Saigon, Vietnam. Fashionable dressed Vietnamese teens sip noodle soup while Thai, Cambodian, Laotian, Burmese, Asian Indian, and Chinese shop for fresh lemongrass, ginger root, and rice. This is also true of Los Angeles, New York, Miami, Montreal, Vancouver and elsewhere. Then there is the French of Quebec. This underlines the need that the gospel should be offered to every language group within their cultural setting. As an individual one may resent intrusions- imagined or real- upon their accepted norms of society and language. But as a Christian and representatives of the church, it must be understood that language is a vital element in everyone's cultural identity. This seems more important when it comes to expressions of worship.

Upon stepping to the front to initiate evangelism into the minority language groups of the community, doors are opened to address the need to provide unity within the church fellowship. Regardless of expressed fears, and though awkwardness must be overcome, successes are being recorded in every area of our fellowship as shared services, participation in common projects, and overviews of the total church program emerges.

Buildings, especially those located in congested big-city environment, are expensive. Purpose for such a facility gives birth to sacrifice and fulfillment as congregations pull together to achieve their dreams. But buildings are constructed to be used!

Growth in most circumstances dictated modification. But let's face it, most of our church windows are dark many nights of the week. It is easy to see a church in these settings with a normal Sunday morning English congregation upon dismissal, stopping to greet the incoming Spanish congregation during intermission. If one should be prone to do so, move to the fellowship hall where the Koreans have had their early morning service, and a mirror reflection of the sanctuary is taking place, but they are greeting the incoming Filipinos. The church is then justified to exist.... It is meeting the need of the community. In view of evangelism, don't you think it is time to surrender the prejudices common to cultural preservation, and move to higher values of human behavior?

Chapter Ten
The Church is a Global Community

'Therefore seeing we have this ministry, as we have received mercy, we faint not!....."

In view of the past chapters that bring into focus what I tend to view as a personal responsibility, today, more than ever before there is a reason to be pleased with progress. The frontiers of multicultural participation in the United Pentecostal Church International can be seen broadening, and new congregations filled with mosaic ethnicity come to birth with constant regularity; California leading the race with an average of nearly one per month over a recent 96 month period. Other cultures are quickly closing the gap and are planting churches.

Many of our multicultural congregations have their beginning as an outreach evangelism of an English speaking congregation. Some of these new congregations operate comfortably and effectively toward permanency within the English administration, while others by mutual support of both cultures, move on to an autonomy. The latter sink their roots deep within the fellowship of the United Pentecostal Church International. Both endeavors are healthy, given proper training and leadership.

Across the fellowship, we are blessed abundantly with innovative officials who not only have provided an active leadership, but have given financial support to the program. With confidence these men open doors leading to the acceptance of ethnic converts in the local church, giving attention to language and cultural needs. This has produced a consequential reaction that is filling the foyers of growing United Pentecostal Churches. The key has been simply to understand that all cultures value their heritage. Very few are those in leadership who are not actively involved in some type of outreach ministry, or inspiring others to become involved.

In one of our districts, a Spanish congregation was given birth in a major city by an English congregation. Soon it became apparent that new facilities would be necessary to house the magnificent growth that resulted. Given approval and support by the English pastor, the fledgling congregation rented a church building at a cost of $1500 monthly. With their more spacious quarters, the congregation was able to continue their rapid growth. Soon packing out that facility, they caught the attention of the district board, who assisted in the purchase of a beautiful church building. They have since modified their new sanctuary three times to keep pace with their successes, and have not only their multicultural language congregation, but an English outreach as well.

Not long ago the district superintendent, a frequent visitor, preached a challenging message that moved the membership to seek refuge in the altar. There they wept with hearts bleeding for their families and countrymen who were without God. The challenge presented the truth that every congregation must have a priority of winning the lost, regardless of culture or language. He added, "Wo one culture since the church's beginning can exert proprietorship over the gospel! The church of the Living God is not limited to the boundaries of culture."

Being present, I was impacted by his appeal, but wept openly as the congregation began to pour out their personal finances onto the altar. Those who had no ready currency, placed an I.O.U. note to identify with the sacrifice. Over $7,000 in cash was realized when the notes were covered. This offering was used to again modify the sanctuary to make room for the growing family.

On another occasion, I accompanied a young ethnic minister as he met his district board to receive his local license. That same year, he rented a building only three blocks from his sectional presbyter who was completely supportive. Since it was a minority language group, there has been absolutely no conflict because of the close proximity. A firm and intimate friendship guides the ethics of these two great men. Not only has the multicultural congregation exploded with new converts, but the English congregation was blessed with an multicultural outreach as well. It is standing room only in the multicultural church on any given service schedule. Last year the congregation raised 13 thousand dollars for missions.

Some Spanish Ministry Examples

In the Los Angeles area, a Spanish bi-monthly rally was held in a local church which doubles for both an English and a Spanish congregation. Both are working together to win their city. With a capacity crowd extending into the foyer of the 600 capacity building, Superintendent Paul Price preached by special invitation. With smiles of satisfaction showing openly upon the faces of those attending, the crowd surged to their feet constantly to respond to the translated message. What a night!

Shortly afterward, the Northern region of California celebrated their Spanish Bimonthly Rally in Fresno's Truth Tabernacle, pastored by Vaughn Morton. Ernest Martinez preached a very inspiring message to the enthusiastic congregation. As I looked over the number of people, I could hardly contain my feelings! These activities are the result of a leadership that is willing to view the world as the field. The United Pentecostal Church is an international church.... reaching the world! Only three years previous to that time, meetings of this nature could have been held in a small capacity auditorium. Now monthly rallies must search for a large capacity church in order to accommodate those who congregate.

That year we had to turn over 100 people away from the scheduled Spanish Family Camp convening at the Sugar Pines Campground. The dorms were filled to over capacity, and the tabernacle packed for the evening services. As a result we had to schedule two annual Spanish camps to accommodate the event.

The Texas District celebrated their Third Annual Spanish Family Camp, and nearly 2,000 were in attendance. Other districts such as The Georgia District have tapped into migrant work camps and have given birth to beautiful Spanish congregations as an extension of the mother church. Pastors in that district who cannot speak Spanish have initiated effective activities merely by the love they demonstrate toward these precious people. Georgia has celebrated their Second Annual Spanish Family Camp.

National Spanish Conferences

It would be difficult to pick out a special Spanish conference and compare it against others. They are all great meetings! However, one comes to mind that propelled the financial support for these meetings.

Our General Superintendent, Nathaniel Urshan, was invited to preach the keynote message during our national scale Spanish conferences. He thrilled the congregation by inserting into his translated message several praises in the Spanish language. The people related well to Brother Urshan, and felt they are a valid part of his leadership. During the Tampa, Florida, conference. Brother Urshan was challenging the Spanish to higher levels of participation and growth. He elicited responses from his hearers that shook the packed auditorium. At one point everything stood still as a powerful move of God hallowed the atmosphere. Young Spanish men- tomorrow's potential leaders of this ministry- actually flung themselves upon the altar to bring Brother Urshan's message to an unplanned culmination. It reminded me of the "afterglow" of Solomon's prayer when the glory of the Lord filled the temple! From that point, the annual conference took on a different meaning.

Also during that conference Lewis Morley, a retired missionary to Colombia, S.A. and former Field Representative for Spanish Ministries, preached a message that expressed his appreciation for the tremendous strides that had been made in Spanish evangelism. Brother Morley was the first coordinator for Spanish Ministries. He encouraged the Spanish ministers to claim the victories promised those who sow the seeds of the gospel.

After the Tampa Spanish Conference, I encountered a very busy schedule researching the Spanish Oneness history following the Azusa Street Revival. I had been asked to highlight the Jesus name message among those of the Spanish culture during the Heritage Conference held in Los Angeles that year. It is noteworthy that in history the Spanish were not influenced by the Trinitarian doctrine, but flowed directly into a "oneness" format. I presented these findings to the conference with enthusiasm.

Evangelism Into The Black Community

As among the Spanish, the United Pentecostal Church is making tremendous strides among those of the black culture. While there are specific overtones of cultural emphasis necessary for the black, there is no language barrier to impede evangelism. The neighborhood church need only open the doors to actively preach the gospel of peace, and willing Black families will be there to accept its benefits. Successful assimilation into the church family will depend upon the attitude each will develope toward the other, and how racial differences will be perceived.

It must be understood that differences exist. The secular world is so full of disdain for many things, and the black seems to be a favorite target. The young Black male has been challenged to produce family values, but the lack of proper employment many times reduces his dream to a dismal failure. The statistics abound that readily speak of the percentages destined to see incarceration, but statistics alone create no viable alternate route. No innovative programs are presented to paint the rosy pictures of a future apart from drugs and alcohol. In the neighborhood he is expected to live up to the media's prediction, and many of them generally do. It is the church that will make the difference.

In the church, where there is no difference in race and culture, a new life is available! The United Pentecostal Church has white pioneer pastors who have created new avenues for the young black male- a minister of the gospel! Whether the congregation becomes autonomous, or whether it remains a part of the white mother church does not seem to matter, evangelism is reaching very successfully into the black community. Love has constructed a strong bridge that spans the once formidable separation, bringing brothers and sisters of the faith together. The secular expectations no longer apply.

Men such as Calvin Enlow, Kenneth Mack, Moses Hightower, Richard Rose, Marvin Bembry, Richard Allman, and Raymond Watson of the American Black; Chester and Michael Mitchell, Trevor Neal, and Oliver Barnes of the Jamaican culture, among countless others thrill our conferences with anointed Holy Ghost ministry. They have proven that no barrier will be tolerated in the family of God.

Working shoulder to shoulder with administration. Multicultural Ministries has provided the coordination of cultural activities, and God has brought into the kingdom the changes that predict a great future. The Annual Evangelism Into The Black Community Conference brings some of the greatest people on earth together. Oneness? You'd better believe it. Those who minister the gospel from the conference pulpit thrill the very heart of God. A living example of holiness, those who attend the annual conference walk the streets in such a manner the business community solicits their cities to invite the conference.

Am I proud? In each conference I find it difficult to believe it can get better- but it does! I am tremendously pleased with the results of Multicultural Ministries, and feel that every facet of our plan has been implemented with unquestionable success.

In a Dallas, Texas, Conference on Evangelism Into The Black Community, Marvin Bembry was a daytime seminar teacher. He spoke eloquently about reaching the "untapped territories," and what we must do to expand our borders. "Pentecost," Brother Bembry said, "was merely a place of beginning. It quickly moved the ministry of the apostles to the street, introducing the church to every nation. It brought into focus the knowledge of one Lord, one faith, and one baptism. Therefore, the church of today is a place where black folks will evangelize people who don't look like them..., but to do that it must move out into the street where hungry people wait."

Another great evangelism message during that conference was preached by Moses Hightower. His words, "If the Blacks target only the Blacks, what about the other 94% of the United States population? It's time somebody breaks down the walls and reaches the world... whoever we are, and whoever "they" are, and wherever "they" may be found." He continued later, "I am not a Black minister, I am a called minister of the gospel. I am called to evangelize the world, not just my kind."

We are only touching the surface of what could be accomplished if all our churches could catch the vision of Multicultural Evangelism. Two or three distinct congregations can utilize the same facility by alternating service schedules. A man can become a powerful pastor as he climbs the social barriers to perform cross-culture evangelism. A pastor with a positive vision, and a will to reach the lost, will find the gospel providing access to culture, and the genuine love he possesses for people will do the rest. It is a myth to think an English speaking pastor cannot meet the challenge. Just ask men who have pioneered this ministry, and who have been involved! Men such as Paul Price, Scottie Teets, O. C. Crabtree, James Kilgore, Jack Yonts, Jack Cunningham, Phil White, Allan Abbey, and others who are among the many officials and pastors who have defeated this myth. With their vision we are bringing to birth within the United Pentecostal Church International a mighty revival among our ethnic communities of North America. The angels in heaven are shouting "Amen!", as the lost of our continent are being reached. Increasingly effective, inroads are being made into every culture through cross-culture evangelism.

The dream of an international end-time revival is touching the fingertips of the United Pentecostal Church International. The church is awakening to the responsibility of discerning the secular from the spiritual when it comes to evangelism. And, because the church is the possessor of the only saving gospel, we must move into the leadership role and create an innovative program that will ignite the total church with the possibilities that been given us. As leaders, we must step to the front and lead our churches into uncharted paths. Part of being a leader is that we cannot continue to merely run with the pack, we must surge ahead into new dimensions.

As cultural groups are introduced into the North American church through the efforts of Multicultural Ministries, we are finding ways to deal with cultural differences. Worshipping the same Lord, and many times in the same church, our variegated congregations are beginning to export revival by their expertise in language and custom.

Smoothing out cultural wrinkles demands more than a casual approach, or even attending a seminar on the subject. To make lasting changes become a reality, rigid goals to destroy discrimination within the Body of Christ must be set. Perhaps the most important factor for this change has come from an unequivocal commitment from every level of the church that God's love transcends all barriers.

Can we learn the secret of that love? Can we preach with fervor that God loves the whole world, yet feel it difficult to speak to our neighbor across the back yard fence? Somewhere we are going to have to take a stand for what is right... and it is right to evangelize our North American continent, even those who are not our kind. We must also assimilate them into our local assemblies even though it may be an arduous task. There will be those who will continue to be racial in the reverse sense, but it is our responsibility to keep trying.

Our missionaries are commissioned to go to other lands and are expected to perform. We support them to do a job too many are unwilling to attempt. They cross over continents of difference in race, culture, and religion, to risk even their lives as they represent a church that many times is spoiled with the better comforts of life. They serve in a place without malls, microwaves, and in many areas, inside toilets. Can we not evangelize those same cultures on the domestic front?

The Bible tells us to love our neighbor. But too often that means our neighbor has to look like us, or think like us, to qualify. When men learn the secret of God's love and serve in Christ's stead, it radically changes our perception of those around us.

Maybe we are too quick to assume that in North America multicultural gulfs can't be bridged. Sometimes they can, sometimes they can't, and in this there's no predicting until we make the attempt- and it can't be proven by one or even a number of failed attempts.

Is it possible that we expect our missionaries to scale international barriers, high walls of social hostility, and produce a result that merits our financial giving, and at home we apologize because we can not adjust an attitude toward those of our continent because they are of another culture?

Relative to our missionaries, maybe we need our emotions pierced with guilt. What makes some go where others who should have, did not? It's difficult to step forward and surrender what many times is a life's work and accept a calling that enters into a constant battle of wills, calling upon tightly wound emotions to keep a balance in the midst of cultural ambiguity and language barriers. In the starting rounds, logic batters the sub-consciousness of many new missionaries until common sense says, "...get out of it quickly, you have made a mistake." But divine calling says, "Stay with it, you are right, and in time the fruit of your labor will bring unbelievable returns." The passing of time has the last word as it looks back over those turbulent times and brings into focus a love for a people culturally different from the missionary, but somehow have woven themselves into the fabric of friendship, and more importantly, a brotherhood.

It is easy to throw up your hands and let those unwilling to accept the Lord's commission without reserve drive spiritual values from you. Why step out of the culture and comfort zone to put body, soul, and spirit on the front line? For me, the earthly ministry of our Lord held the answer. He called upon men to forsake all and follow Him. He declared, "The foxes have holes, and the birds of the air have their nests; but the Son of man hath not where to lay his head." There comes a time when the need becomes so great we take our stand for something, no matter the risk. Maybe, just maybe, the choice will not be difficult to make when we once more study the life of Christ and be energized by his love.

When it comes to His ministry, Jesus is best explained in the Book of Acts. It simply states that He "went about doing good." As He drew near the end of His earthly ministry, he explained to His followers that "...greater things than these shall ye do..." That He based these results upon the increased numbers of disciples involving themselves in the ministry, is a foregone conclusion. The church- His body on the earth- would continue the important work of reconciling men unto God. It was upon this important principle the church was established.

The Church provides a refuge for a weary, sin tossed world. Sinners, tired of the grief given birth by the many upheavals of a lifestyle void of God, find peace within its walls. For it is there that happiness replaces depression, and singing drives the tears far from eyes accustomed to weeping. This is a common story among believers who long have possessed a background of a saving Christ, but only recently in North America have countless others been introduced to His saving grace.

Today the United Pentecostal Church is enjoying the growth of a new generation of believers. They too, have found new life, and the fabulous truth they have embraced includes a complete change from everything they have ever known! They are the Asians who in the past worshiped many gods, including lifeless images formed of inanimate materials. Their lifestyle also involved ancestor worship where family traditions had no intimacy nor interest in a crucified Christ.

Just as the church becomes a melting pot of a cross-section of humanity emerging from many denominational traditions, the United Pentecostal Church is experiencing a great revival sweeping the west coast. This revival is resulting in a complete change of face from the accepted norm of yesterday's results. Demographic changes constantly altering set patterns have influenced greatly the genetic amalgamation taking place. It is not surprising to hear several languages as the sounds of prayer fill a local church sanctuary. Neither is it surprising to see representatives of as many as four or five cultures who have already assimilated into the spiritual family, assisting a new convert in the altar, each worshipping in the language of his birth.

Daniel Robinson, an Apache Indian born on the White Mountain Apache Reservation, was taken to the Orlando Florida Detention Center for some domestic infraction. It was not a mere casual contact, but an outreach ministry of the Apopka United Pentecostal Church that brought Daniel face to face with a new life. Under a very controlled agreement with the officials of the Center, the Apopka church provides a bus to bring detainees to the church services. When Daniel came in contact with the spirited worship of the Apopka United Pentecostal Church, immediately he decided that this was the life he wanted. The church's productive outreach guided Daniel to repentance, and Pastor Michael Williams requested me to baptize him in the name of Jesus Christ. That night Daniel received the Holy Ghost and I saw the possibilities of an outreach to the Apache Nation. He has been involved in Home Bible Study for several months, and my prayer is, that his future will bring honor and glory to God among his own people.

For those wishing to experience a return on missionary dollars spent from Foreign Missions giving. There is a story of two brothers, products of missionary endeavors in Ecuador, South America. Josias Limones married my daughter, Neva, and upon our return to the States, established a Spanish speaking church in the city of Borger, Texas.

Initiating Spanish services in the facilities of Bethel Tabernacle, the Spanish congregation quickly moved into an adequate rented facility due the rapid growth of the congregation. Josias worked the parks where Spanish families gathered after working hours and on the week-ends, and provided a jail ministry for the local inmates.

A Baptist church building was going to ruin. The denomination who had occupied the building had long since abandoned holding church services, and it had become a warehouse for old refrigerators, freezers, and air conditioners. When Josias requested to buy the property, the Texico District Home Missions Department said, "...it's not worth the effort!" Josias felt the call of God emanating from that place, and financed the purchase from his own pocket. District officials during the dedication ceremonies were amazed as they looked upon the miraculously transformation. Today there is an absolutely wonderful congregation inhabiting one of the most beautiful facilities we have in Spanish Ministries. Two daughter Spanish churches have been given birth in neighboring communities.

The brother, Elias Limones, came to live in the United States. After a time of development assisting his brother, Josias Limones, in Borger, he then moved to Concord, California. Seeing the need of evangelizing the Spanish of North America, he felt led to request of his pastor, Garland Verdier, to allow him to utilize the facilities of Calvary Apostolic Church of Concord, and initiate services in the Spanish language. Within weeks the sanctuary was packed with hungry Spanish converts. Pastor Verdier was proud of the Spanish speaking daughter church, and assisted in finding the congregation a suitable location. After various moves, including several months holding services in a public park, the congregation now hold title to their own beautiful place of worship. The magnificent growth continued until numerous modifications have been made necessary in the existing building. As many as 400 have crowded into the sanctuary, signaling that time again has arrived to seek new floor space. Several English speaking families bring the church to a full circle, and bi-lingual services are celebrated by necessity.

Adrian Santos and his wife, Hyde, came to Deltona, Florida, with their family. An emerging minister of Puerto Rico, he felt the call to evangelize the many Spanish converging onto Florida from Puerto Rico and Cuba. Establishing his services first in the homes of believers, he them moved to a Presbyterian church located in the same city. Paying an astronomical cost for this facility, he prayed constantly for the church to acquire the proper location to sink its roots.

The Deltona Corporation, a building and developing company, approached Brother Santos about constructing a church building on property where they were planning a development. The venture would include a donation of land upon which the new facility would be constructed, and the church would provide the Deltona Corporation a promotion for the new community. The only restriction for the acreage was that an approved sanctuary would dominate the landscape within one year. That sounded easy!

My first responsibility as coordinator for Spanish Ministries was to travel to Deltona and assess the merits of this venture. The General Home Missions Division had allocated fifteen thousand dollars to assist in the construction of the new church. Contracts were reviewed to ascertain that no future claim could emerge against the district due the church's affiliation with the UPCI. The property was investigated and found to be a prime parcel of real estate valued at $105,000 in its undeveloped state. When the investigation was completed, it was ascertained to be without problem, and the signing of documents was promptly conducted.

The easy part was quickly put behind us as the three responsibilities were accomplished. The hard part was to bring cultural understanding to a satisfactory conclusion. The distance between the Florida District Board and the Spanish congregation was a learning experience. The success of this was realized when retired Colombian missionary, Lewis Morley and I were able to bring all the factors together, and the documents signed to protect the GHMD investment in a home mission project.

Under the careful guidance of newly elected Superintendent O C. Crabtree, we put together a financing package for the construction of the building, a retired contractor to over see the project, and a dedication service that filled the beautiful new facilities.

At present. Brother Santos has enlarged the facility by constructing an addition to provide Sunday School rooms and a fellowship hall. Another success story for Spanish Ministries.

These stories have the ability to reproduce themselves time and again, if we will take the time to reflect upon the possibilities. Across the United States and Canada, how many new churches could be constructed with a little assistance in understanding. Finances are not the deciding factor! Our ethnic cultures need camaraderie and acceptance. With knowledge that a church family is there for assistance in traversing the many obstacle courses a person of another culture faces in a strange environment, they can walk the distance.

This doesn't seem like much of a responsibility, but it takes time and patience, and most of all a willingness to put yourself in their place. Your missionaries do it every day, and report great victories as cultural barriers are broken. Will we do it? Yes, I believe we will. We will because it is right, because it is a part of our commitment to God, and because we desire to evangelize the world. The result of our efforts will be a global community with local responsibilities.

Chapter Eleven
Evangelism Into The Black Community

There is no doubt the church is influenced by secular trends. Invariably, what society deems correct has a bearing on what the church deems correct. And, whether that is right or wrong depends on the issue itself. However, for the spiritual values of developing Christians to be shaped with clarity, and the proper mentality maintained in the light of social acceptance, the scales of values upon which the church judges right and wrong must be derived from biblical principles.

The Bible transcends every cultural barrier, and without respect to a particular culture guides each to the higher principles God infused into mankind in the beginning. Thus we are to conclude that He expects us to develop proper attitudes according to HIS principles, and not become influenced by what society has caused to evolve and call it correct.

As we take a look at the scriptures we learn that the earth is the Lord's and the fullness thereof, and all they that dwell therein. This is a solid truth established from the mind of God, and excludes no one.

That men have debilitated the values produced by God for humanity is easily understood. From the time of his first error, man has felt secure in his ability to figure out what is best for his particular involvement. That his outlook is filled with prejudice, and therefore biased, does not seem to matter, only that he benefits from any given results. With that thought in mind, we can readily understand why social patterns have fallen into moral decay, and why the judgment of any dominant society may very well perpetuate the preservation of their mentality.

Perhaps no generation has ever been as confused as our present one. Neither has there been a previous generation that has developed so much potential for convenience, comfort, and preservation, as has this present generation. They have learned to fly in the air like a bird. They have developed skill to swim beneath the water as a fish, but they have never learned to walk the earth as a man.

Therefore, please allow me the privilege of investigating root causes, and let's establish a few possible steps we might take to bring about a blending of the world's cultures into the church. Without judging the right or wrong thought pattern, let the reader and the writer bring to the front even the most touchy issues, and from that point produce the better environment by a process of elimination.

In the secular world, trends have been set by years of racial bias. Mentality has been programmed by the accepted norm of a present society. One must understand that each generation is not a product of itself, rather the product of the previous generation. The actions and teachings of values of that generation were predicated upon what they had been taught. How sad that negative emotions have been so difficult to dislodge when it relates to such an important, and indispensable, item as racial acceptance.

The deep south of the past was forged to consider the Black as less than human and not a counterpart in the game of life. This bias began in the days of slavery, a despicable slice of history best left forgotten on the shelves of our nation's chronicles. The mentality was passed on as a legacy to children who were taught to raise walls of separation between the cultures, and time has produced a major glitch in the minds of otherwise productive persons who forged the direction for their generation.

An example of this was introduced by a professional writer... "When I was a trainee with IBM in New York in the late 1950s, the head instructor apologized to us Southern trainees because two of her instructors were black!"[1] It appears that the contact might have been too much for the Southern trainees. This type of perpetual stigma is a signal for others to imitate, and thus the mentality is solidified.

The era of slavery was ended by the refusal of the white society to place their approval upon such bigotry, and preferred to die on a battlefield rather than allow others of their race to continue a practice that polarized the nation. The thousands of young men who died on the battlefields of a war that produced shame and sorrow for a great nation, were young men who had productive lives ahead of them. There was more bloodshed in the Civil War than in both World Wars combined. Add the Korean War, and the Vietnam War, and you still have a lower figure. Those who died should have been in colleges and universities preparing for careers such as lawyers and doctors. Instead they defended the right of all men to be equal, and have a right to the pursuit of happiness. They did not die in vain. What they did returned honor and dignity to a great people, and repaired the breeches marring the foundation of their values.

However, the results of history create culture where all men become prisoners of the experiences of time. What we are doing today in the seemingly insignificant activities we involve ourselves in, is forging the history others will read. To free ourselves from the unfavorable mentalities created by the events of yesteryear, we must move outside of the accepted norm and make a greater impact upon society. We must carefully plan adjustments that will bring changes for good, and replace undesirable tendencies that have not guided decision making values in the proper direction.

Society is in a constant mode of change. Nothing stays the same. Things that great men of today's world are doing are soon replaced by greater minds who have become more efficient because they learned from the mistakes of the past. The ideas that great men thought yesterday are considered juvenile by the evolved principles of change. Thank God the world is reshaping its concepts as they relate to racial values.

That which emerged out of history forced certain people to retreat into themselves for protection and preservation of culture. Every culture loves the values produced by their predecessors. This is what they are, and each has considerable wealth to contribute to the overall picture. In this manner the black fed positive threads into a loom that produced a fabric of moral fiber sufficient to carry their people through the long days and short nights of severe suffering, not the least that of mental anguish. That they could not simply step out of their world even for a moment to adjust direction was beyond comprehension. The prison walls were simply too confining. Surrender to the insurmountable powers of their times drove them into churches to sing of a better day. Dreams were easy to embrace because they had perimeters of happier experiences. Their songs took on a far deeper emotion than actualities, and gave perpetual power to take them for the moment out of the sadness of the hour. All too soon the real world would return, but the song remained as a mental force to drive them to a better day. Too many died without realizing that new day.

The black culture is gregarious and creates a structure dealing with spiritual values. That in itself inspires mental challenges. It is emotive and energetically expressive. That is why black orators were able to promote solidarity. When the dream was embraced by an effective orator, it was perpetuated by others who took up the theme.

Terrence Roberts, a black psychologist from Los Angeles, teaches families how to deal effectively with racism and, as Christians, how to forgive. On one occasion, he said, "The unique part of being an African-American, is you are forced to put racism on the agenda for the education of your children.

"The theater, television, and real live drama stereotypes the image of African-Americans, and picked up by the media, portrays such a picture that most black parents look at and say, "None of our children are those things!" The children cannot attend a movie or sit through a television program dealing with blacks without wondering if they are indeed Black because they do not fit the negative stereotype."[2]

When news stories conclude that all Black males somehow fit in a pattern, there are reproductive influences that indicate to many young Black males that they should create the image, if indeed it is not already taking shape in their mind.

It is extremely important in light of heightened racial tensions that a proper mentality guide people through problems created by those tensions. Racial loyalty suggests that emotions should rest on the side of compatriots, and that like kind should stick together. This is particularly true when hyped up situations produce wrong decisions.

The key to fighting racism is for parents to nourish a self-respect in their children for other people who may be different. That young people are educated to what racism is all about, and how to separate what is going on around them from what they are, and that they personally are not the cause. Then they should judge fairly to what degree others are guilty in the light of the evidence and adjudicate individual guilt, and not merely to resolve social debate.

It must be established that injustice has two sides to the expendable coin. Sometimes it is a measure of just how badly politicians have failed in putting together a social structure that could really work, and thus racial problems are merely passed on to the next set of activities that will once again ignite sparks of heated debate rather than settle the question once and for all. The social system that we are a part of today must not be subverted by side issues, but all of us must put together a mechanism that functions, and will operate for our children to grow up in. Racial politics do not properly address racial tensions, because politicians endeavor to wring every ounce of leverage from circumstances that can induce people to agree with them, thus propelling their personal agendas for personal benefit.

Parents of both white and African-American children should explain that racism is something the American people have inherited, and many times is used to confuse real issues based in economics and social class struggles. Comprehension will come when root causes are understood, and adjusted.

Black is a culture that exists, preaching black supremacy. In frustration many young black males are carried downstream by this mentality, and are swallowed in the sarcasm emanating from the resulting hatred. But somehow the church must create a new category depicting understanding that we are all in a state of survival, and need to co-exist as diverse cultures striving to succeed for our families, and indeed, the future of all mankind. The key will be to excite young black men in existing churches by providing special training that will eliminate the influence of secular exclusivism. White pastors must take the initiative and create quality black men to assume leadership roles, allowing them to step to the front in high visibility, thus providing for the emerging black youth, a model example worthy of imitating. This would play a double role. It would also teach our upcoming white youth that cultural differences do not exclude those who strive to excel.

The other extreme of African-American children's confusion, is the hatred generated by white supremacist groups. Misguided parents who speak in the presence of their children about racial superiority, add to the problem in such a way that years down the road that child yet feels the results of such scales of value. It is wrong to believe that one culture is superior to another.

It is the dominant culture in any nation that shapes national life. The threads of humor, music, food, dress, art, science, literature, and most importantly, history, is that which produces the mentality of the present generation. For America, it is wrong to believe the dominant culture is a white culture. It is loaded with African, Hispanic, Asian, and mixed with white Irish, German, and other European values. The mix comes because people mix. It is inevitable. Cultural objects that have appeal are adopted into the mainstream, both the negative and the positive. But people have to accept one another, to touch shoulders, and thereby influence society to what is right, what is good, and what is better. Otherwise the uncontrolled, dynamic and adaptive, will provide what confronts the issues, and the results passed to the emerging generation who has no power over what they inherit.

The melting pot served for many years, but true America, and I believe the American majority, is ready for the stew pot where everyone adds to the flavor without losing the characteristics of culture or personality.

Racial progress came with a price. It was the hard work of the silent majority that made possible the results of the emerging positives for the new generation being given birth. After decades of struggle and achievement, Black children of the turbulent generation were secure enough to pursue their own ideals and desire without the dragging weights of color. It would, and did, take time to heal the wounds caused by distrust and hate. The two merged together into a marriage that produced the most enduring changes inside the hearts and minds of individual Americans. The resulting impact said, "Enough!" It then released a backlash that dominated reason for the cause and effect that energized the generation that followed.

We today, experience a brotherhood that is void of the roots of prejudice, even though some of the fruit yet exists from the shadows of the past. There has never been a better time to get on with this business of evangelism. Our churches have become heirs of a wealth produced by the generations who suffered to make it a reality. Therefore, we must not be irresponsible with this legacy, but we must invest this wealth wisely and it will produce for those who will follow our example.

In the United Pentecostal Church today we can see an open display of camaraderie among the races, so we need to build upon the friendship that it implies, stepping to the doors of new dimensions of evangelism. We can do it if we try. The Black in the United Pentecostal Church International is a reality that brings security for all of us. Every time we see a black face in our conferences, or every time a black minister stands at the podium to minister, it represents the fact that we have survived all those painful battles, and have carved a victory out of the chaos. The answer now is to move on to the mentality that racial diversity is common to us, and show the world that the church holds the key to destroying hostilities that exist among people.

We can work at every level to develop a relationship that will address the challenges faced by those struggling to gain a personal relationship with God, and destroy forever the negatives that were once commonplace in time. No entity apart from the church has such a breadth of experience gained by bucking the views of the masses. We do it because it is godly, and because we represent Him.

The landscape of any history becomes the epitome of its future. No one can remain suspended in time. Those who would excel must master the changes constantly being made, if control is ever to be exerted over turmoil. The church must adjust to a changing world while it clings to a changeless truth, and assume whatever level of responsibility necessary for the results of evangelism. The church will do this because it is the embodiment of He who came to reconcile all men to God.

As a church we will not look to crisis intervention as the answer to the ills that befall us. We must look at the long-term wealth of a good attitude if we expect to see a difference in the way people treat one another. We must redefine ourselves as we expect others to redefine themselves. We are the church, and we provide the spiritual food for families to grow on. We provide education substance necessary for survival. We meet the need for good to dominate the mentality of our fellowship. Therefore, we will vehemently oppose even one convert being neglected, abused, or left to the mercy of this evil generation. The youth especially must receive the bulk of our attention in order to implant the seeds of expectancy. Black youth is a fertile soil into which we will cultivate a future filled with confidence. They, and all youth, derive their values from the basics taught from example.

Success stories produce facts that will blur our vision of the past, and sharpen our focus upon the future. Like a wise master builder, we must, and will, destroy all that stands in the way of this new day, and add to our faith an astonishing capacity to assimilate our knowledge and translate it to reason.

We have catapulted from a divided world into a new world capable of fulfilling the great commission. We are limited only by refusing to take advantage of our capacities emanating from the evolving factors of the past. Simple miscalculations can frustrate our grandest and most viable opportunity for world evangelism since Pentecost. A fantasy world energized by personal attitudes will exact negative results for inventive progress and produce a price tag we can ill afford.

However cherished the love of God, it will not break down the barriers to abolish old hatreds connected to racial, ethnic or nationalistic differences. Neither can it dispense with religious fanaticism nor self-righteousness that accompanies an attitude that is narrower than God's character. We must desperately reach for new futures... new frontiers that will justify the sacrifices of our spiritual forefathers, and provide reason for those who are the heirs of their examples. By God's help we shall not retreat into old boundaries of hatred, distrust, and separatism. God has given us the opportunity for an endless quest, and with it an infinite wealth to open worlds never before imagined possible.

Therefore, the fantasy of a flawless future is not the mentality to embrace. There is no such thing as a perfect world apart from heaven itself. Yet we must dream, but there will be questions which the dream, as dreams often do, will leave for the participants to answer. The task is our's, and our's alone. How will we accomplish the responsibility? How will the total world be evangelized before Jesus comes? I simply do not know the answers to either of those questions, but we must climb every hill, and cross every river that stands between us and the objective. We shall because we, you and I together, are the church!

There will be some unconverted people who still show disdain for the black, and who will continue to demonstrate this terrible injustice. The same will be true on the black side of the question. But in the church, let's get on with saving our young black men by planting new energies, new dreams, and new professions into the fertile soils of change. God can call a black to minister to his kind- or any kind- and make him productive for the Kingdom of God. Since there is a vast need for role models among the black culture that will guide the emerging youth from the streets, the church must produce this model, and activate a confidence that there will be opportunities to succeed.

To be a mediator, one must have both natures. He can then relate to both sides, representing each to the other. To be partial is to fail in the attempt. Therefore, we must step to the front and initiate whatever change necessary to tear down the barriers, and that today.

Footnotes:

[1] USA Today - August 23, 1993 - N. Berry
[2] San Gabriel Tribune - August 24, 1993 - Terrence Roberts

Chapter 12
The Asian Revival

Like a slowly swinging door that provides entrance to the migratory masses, the United States and Canada have been turning around during the last century. A continent that once looked to Europe is now turning its face toward Asia. The consequences of this shift for every area of the United Pentecostal Church International are enormous.

For nearly 2000 years the Christian church has struggled to share the gospel in Asia. Luke, in fact, records the first setback: the Apostle Paul's dramatic left turn into Europe, "...having been forbidden by the Holy Ghost to preach the word in Asia..." (Acts 16:6). Perhaps the Holy Ghost was guiding Paul to develop key preaching points in Europe that would become launching pads for future propagation of the gospel. For if the gospel could take root in those key preaching points, it would radiate throughout Europe, and from Europe to the whole world. This is exactly what happened, starting from the Greek speaking city of Ephesus in West Asia.[1] But what about the Asia populace? Is it time now? Has God reserved the greatest Asian revival for our time? If so, the responsibility that precedes the opportunity is tremendous. The church must adjust its evangelism strategy to have the greater success, and to weave the subsequent results into a one church concept. Our early church fathers had the same problems, but having overcome them, enjoyed a multi-cultural growth that was fused into a purpose for evangelism.

Throughout the history of the church the progress of the gospel to the Asian has been painfully slow. In our day, the United Pentecostal Church has penetrated the Philippines and India with miraculous results, thanks to some great missionary personnel who have established inroads to a positive revival mentality. Yet we smuggle Bibles to the interiors of a continent where nearly one-half the world's population live, and who are waiting for the gospel.

In this, perhaps we have been interpreting God's direction wrongly. While we are struggling to get inside Asia, God has been moving Asians out of their homelands and into the centers of nearly every large city of North America. China, largely atheist, cannot be touched by normal evangelism. It is doubtful if a Western missionary will ever impact China to the degree of sufficient results where numbers are compared relative to population and converts. But a Chinese? Chinese people living outside China (60 percent of which live on the West Coast of North America), would be one of the largest nations on earth! While the United Pentecostal Church has invested large sums of money to preach the gospel in Asia with relative little results (in comparison to the masses), Asians have quietly, at their own expense, moved to the proximity of the gospel. Could the United Pentecostal Church be on the verge of one of the greatest moves God has ever provided the church - an Asian Pentecost? The results in the form of converts, in my opinion, would return to distant homelands and literally turn the country to Christ- again, at their own expense.

I propose to you that God has designed the Western District, and the Districts of Oregon, Washington, and British Columbia, to witness a move unprecedented in the chronicles of church history. By removing the period from the last sentence of the Book of Acts and replacing it with a comma, we continue to record church history. We are still the church, and by this church God will evangelize that part of the world by strategically moving tomorrow's key personnel into contact with the gospel today. They will return and do a work no Western missionary could ever do: reach into every large city of Asia, or into any given Asian community of every large city outside Asia, as a modern day apostle for the same strategic reasons he chose the cities of Europe in the first century. Using language and culture as tools of evangelism, Asia can be reached. However, we must be prepared to modify our strategies, and loose those who become involved for this thrust. We must relax some few negative apprehensions about foreign cultures, and begin thinking church family, where we are all participants of His great grace.

Today Asia has two-thirds of the world's population, while Europe has only six percent. The shift is not only economical but cultural as well. The countries listed as the Asian Pacific Rim, Japan, China, Korea, Hong Kong, and the Philippines, speak more than 1,000 languages and have the most varied religious and cultural traditions in the world.[2]

Los Angeles, California

The North American Pacific Rim, consisting of the major cities of the west coast, are bulging at the proverbial seams with representatives of those cultures en masse. Los Angeles, for instance, already the second-largest city in the United States, will soon surpass New York. I believe Los Angeles' time has come. The only serious competition for Los Angeles is Seattle, Washington, as the Asian cultural center for North America. Whatever develops, the United Pentecostal Church must come to grips to evangelize the masses that are entering these two major cities. San Francisco, which houses the past Asian masses, is still thinking in the mentality of a by-gone era. Not that it is not important, but the strategy to reach the new Asian must be, and will be, fine-tuned if we are to be successful.

In the past ten years, Greater Vancouver, British Columbia, Canada, has experienced an unprecedented influx of immigrants from Hong Kong in particular, Taiwan and other parts of Southeast Asia, so that the Asian population in Greater Vancouver has now exceeded 300,000- making up almost 25 percent of the city's population.[3]

These immigrants have brought with them wealth, talents and other gifts and resources which greatly benefit Canada. But they have also brought with them new identities, values and lifestyles which often conflict with those that already exist. The most important conflict is religion. This is also true for Los Angeles, Seattle, and other major cities where Asians are now migrating. It is also true where the immigrants from the Middle East are settling.

There are 1,100 mosques and Islamic centers, 1,500 Buddhist centers and 800 Hindu temples located in the United States.[4] California has gleaned the greater population of Cambodians, Massachusetts, the Muslims, and Texas the Hindus. Cities that are generally accepted as very common to most, have a religious landscape that most of its people don't know about. In fact the transformation has been so subtle it has escaped the notice of the masses.

Usually it is a practical matter: a Muslim group will buy a former school and use the gymnasium as the prayer room, so the neighbors drive by without noticing the change. The danger in all this is how will these changes affect America - and how will being in America change them? Good question. The fact is the church must affect these people with the gospel more than they will affect their adopted country.

Some signs are already evident that they wish to affect this nation with their dogmas. Hindus, Sikhs and Muslims have started summer camps. Many have pieced together national advocacy organization. One, the Islamic Society of North America, says there are 8 million Muslims. No matter the exactness of that estimation, the fact remains that these are new Americans that have brought distinctively Asian and Islamic traditions to this country, and most Americans do not realize their nation is evolving from its Judeo-Christian roots. What must happen is that a genuine concern rise from the church pew and begin affecting people with a truth that will cast down pagan values before they have had time to take root in the minds of youth. If sincere efforts are made, every Dagon god will fall in submission with the great God of heaven.

Harmonizing these cultural differences and resolving actual or potential conflicts remains an important task for the community. Among the priorities of the many initiatives that need to be taken seriously, is the church's role in seizing the opportunity to mold new methodology. By allowing the new Asian the liberty of retaining his culture in the secular sense as the productive missionary does in every part of the world, the church can capture the lead even over government agencies using education by workshops, classes, conferences and giving cross-cultural orientation. Of course, it is understood that biblical principles will never be compromised. In other words, the church becomes a bridge to the community and gleans converts that will evangelize this new world.

This should pose no serious problem for the church. We merely step back and adjust our mentality to embrace change, and the results will justify the sacrifices it exacts from us.

The Chinese population in the United States was only 812,178 in 1980. By 1990 it had more than doubled to 1,654,000, mostly residing in Southern California. To a degree the old Chinatowns of yesteryear have been surpassed. New Chinese communities, a more sophisticated cultural entity, are being raised in suburban setting, surrounded by Anglo residents and with a greater infiltration of Chinese. The move has been so subtle the Anglo community has only recently become aware of the transformation.

This new element represents one-fifth of the world's population! This translates to opportunity at our fingertips.[5]

There is no room for fantasy about turning the Asian culture into a Christian community. It will take work and dedication to harmonize biblical principles within the culture if we are to be successful. We are not talking about a few scattered people, we are talking about nearly one-half of the world's population! We must begin to create a North American church that will have neither Jew nor Greek, bond or free, rich or poor as a dominant factor, and may I say, Chinese or English. We are commissioned to evangelize the world, not just North America. If I might be permitted to express a fault of the United Pentecostal Church without offense, we have failed to reach the Asian because we have been too closed. The church has raised cultural walls to cut off many other societies. To properly apply the opportunities God is extending to us, we must step outside our church doors and make our missionary efforts more diverse, and put into practice what so many consider a preaching sermon. The whole world is the whole world, not just a corner of it. We are citizens of heaven while residing on the earth, and particularly in North America. Evangelism is our purpose for existing as a church, and our only business is people. We must rise to a greater challenge to evangelize the Asian now residing in North America. With the economy emphasizing the Pacific Rim, the church can benefit from the exposure.

The Asian has created the greatest responsibility for the church since Pentecost, and we must take advantage of it as an opportunity. Instead of lamenting our task, let us step to the cutting edge of evangelism and take the initiative into willing hands and save the world. The Asian measures truth by who says it. In other words, their very culture would revolve around the embodiment of Truth. It is easy to take their culture and religious training in ancestor worship and turn it around to preach Christ as the embodiment of the Father.

As threatening as the uncertainties and changes have produced for the new society, there are many positive implications. We, as soul-winners, must arm ourselves with a strong message of faith, a loyalty to the high principles of godliness, and sharpen our sickles as we gear up for the greatest revival North America has ever experienced. The United Pentecostal Church International, and in specific, the districts of the Pacific coast, can be the center of this exploding spiritual change. We must set new values, establish new judgment systems, and balance the possibilities against any sacrifice it might exact from us. I believe the possibilities far outweigh any cost that might be levied. What would the Apostle Paul advise if he were here with us today? My guess is that he would take advantage of this key that has been placed in our hands. So let's open the door and step into a new world of revival- the Asian revival! The Western District stands at a threshold of limitless potential, and that will be a big factor for the big picture as it relates to a worldwide revival. The district has prayerfully considered the objectives, and endeavoring to bring into focus the vision God is projecting for the future. To this moment we have been successful in our efforts to mesh these minority cultures with the system, but the end is not yet! Other languages are waiting and available to us in this very diverse district.

With a tremendous revival now taking place in our churches where Asian constituents are congregating, the truth of the One Church Concept is emerging. Mostly a people without a Christian background, they are facing a two-pronged persecution: within their own family where tradition is a strong characteristic, and the church where their culture is just now being understood.

Stockton, California was a seed bed for future revival. With the invitation of one small Hmong child to Christian Life's Sunday school, there was a tidal wave of reaction from among her family and peers. The next Sunday the bus was jammed with precious people who were seeking out someone to love them. It seemed right somehow that the right attitude would be found in the church- and it was! Today that church has baptized well over two thousand of the Asian community living in the city. They are now reaching the second generation of these families.

Robert Thompson, a minister working out of Fresno's Truth Tabernacle, has learned the difficult Hmong language, and established a very effective evangelism program in that city.

From the Hmong people, the evangelism of Asian constituents leaped the cultural barrier into the Cambodian and Lao communities. Effective ministers have been produced that are spearheading the Asian evangelism program.

During a Special Ministries Asian rally convening in Merced, California, Cher Pao Vang and Teng Vang appealed for their people living by the thousands in Thailand. All along the Mekong River, this people have existed for centuries. They are a language group more than a national people. Having been a minority grouping suffering great persecution from their native China, they immigrated to a less explosive surrounding. While the United Pentecostal Church has a powerful missions program for Thailand, the gospel has never penetrated the Hmong people.

The rally was moved to compassion, and funding of these men making a missionary trip to Thailand was approved. Within three weeks, ancestor altars were dragged to the streets and burned... men and women found their personal experience with God as Cher and Teng led them through the new birth process. Baptized in the name of Jesus Christ and filled with the Holy Ghost, the people from six villages established six new congregations that were turned over to the superintendent of Thailand's United Pentecostal Church family.

Further, the Hmong family has expanded to several other districts. The immigration trail has taken beautiful church families to Rhode Island, Wisconsin and North Carolina.

Multicultural Ministries has been a structure through which the Asians can motivate their evangelism program . There is an assurance that the One Church Concept is an overwhelming success as it relates to assimilating Asian constituents into the church family.

Footnotes:

[1] International Urban Associates - Ray Bakke, Executive Director
[2] Megatrends "2000" - John Naisbitt, William Morrow Publishers, 1990
[3] Megatrends "2000" - John Naisbitt, William Morrow Publishers, 1990
[4] Chinese in North America, November-December, 1992
[5] Chinese in North America - November-December, 1992

Chapter Thirteen
Evangelism to the
North American Native Indian Culture

As a consequence of Native American evangelism, there are 2,048 local churches, congregations, or missions under the supervision of 42 denominations, including 164 independent churches. These had a collective membership of 79,219, or an average of 36.8 members per congregation. The total Native American estimated population stands at 1.8 million living on reservations, and 640,367 living in urban areas, but who list their race as Native American.

To mention a few, broken down per major denomination, the average size congregation is: Southern Baptist Convention 95.6, United Church of Christ 62.5, The Episcopal Church 62.0, The Assemblies of God 60.4, The Christian Reformed 59.3, The Pentecostal Church of God 56.0, The Church of the Nazarene 48.7, and The Christian Missionary and Alliance 38.0. The United Pentecostal Church was not listed in any of the records I studied (but it will be, God willing). The churches that are growing rapidly in the areas of multicultural density, are those who have adjusted evangelism strategies to include a more positive attitude toward native culture. The Native American is a proud citizen, and with time develops a beautiful loyalty for the church and its teaching.

Categorized By Tribes

To name a few categories: The Lumbee population situated mainly in North Carolina, is from 26,000 to 30,000. The majority of Lumbee Christian community belongs to the Southern Baptist Convention which have 48 congregations, 57 ordained ministers and 52 licensed ministers, all Lumbee. The average church congregation numbers 121.6. The largest congregation is the Lumbee Methodist Church in Maxton, NC, with a membership of 670.

Arapahos are generally American Baptists and Pentecostals, while the Caddos are Methodists and Southern Baptists. Geronimo's Chiricahua Apaches are Reformed, American Baptists and Pentecostal. The Shawnee embraces the Southern Baptist Convention; The Otoe-Missouria find their spiritual home among the Pentecostals; the Pawnee belong to the Catholic and the Methodist, while the Poncas lean toward the Nazarene. The Wyandottes are Friends.

The Apaches, once the destroyers of the settlements, have begun to accept the Christian Faith. The White Mountain Apaches of the Fort Apache Reservation in Arizona have 13 churches with about 1,000 members, and their neighbors of the San Carlos Reservation have 7 congregations with more than 725 members. The Jicarilla Apaches have 3 churches with only a few more than 100 members; the Mescaleros of New Mexico have also 3 churches with 189 members.

The Hopis in Northern Arizona have been impervious to even a veneer of Christianity, while the Navajos, who surround them entirely have since 1960 shown receptivity toward the Christian Faith. The Navajos who form the largest Native American grouping, living on the nation's largest reservation, exerts a great power of attraction for missionaries and evangelists to work among them. The greatest successes as it relates to evangelism, is found in the areas where the minister is indigenous, no matter how impervious that area had been previous to the new concept. The indigenous Navajo ministers are forging the results of evangelism into small close-knit churches, and producing ministers who are able to communicate the gospel in the Navajo language.

The Dakotas or Sioux are the largest Christian community among the Northern Plains Indians. Their membership is divided among some ten denominations. Here again it is noteworthy that the growth has been attributed to the fact that the ministry of the gospel is in the vernacular language.

The Native Alaskan churches are growing more receptive to the gospel. Their people are distinctly different than most of the Native Americans of the lower 48 states. The Aleuts and Eskimos are not Indians. The Athabascan peoples are Indian. The American Lutheran Church, Evangelical Covenant, and the California Friends have old and strong Eskimo churches, as do the Moravians. Eleven church denominations which work among the Eskimos have 127 churches with a 20,000 membership. Eight groups work among the Athabascan peoples in 67 churches.

The Background

One of the chapters men would like to see erased from history, belongs to the American Indian of the United States, and the First Nation Residents of Canada. Possibly that era of time was taken out of focus because of the shame and embarrassment it sheds upon the forefathers of these great nations, and the guilt it still creates for the descendants of those who so cruelly and heartlessly exiled a noble people from their beloved homeland. I hope by once again exploring history people who were formerly unaware of the sadness it produced for the Indian, will know the truth, and will weep themselves as they go back in history to experience the pain and heart break of those who found it difficult to understand changing society.

One such experience was the saga of the Cherokee and their forced removal to the Indian Territory. Having title to their properties did little to stem the tide of determined men who lusted after their lands. That journey was known by the Cherokee as The Trail of Tears. History has a way of intruding upon the present, and truth will prevail. There remains a need in all of us to become so emotionally shocked that it will produce a need to study the past with a greater sense of duty in order to gain a better focus on the future.

Such a study would produce a clear and contrasting picture taken from a different angle. The United Pentecostal Church wishes to evangelize the American Indian! Just how much history will qualify our need to modify our approach to them, will depend upon how impartial we judge credibility in the balances of our own feelings of cultural superiority.

A candid study will reveal that the Indians were human beings, good, bad, and indifferent, just as any society before them, and certainly the society that followed. They were people who lived, coping with harsh environments, without more than limited interchanges with other tribal groups, and without outside help at all.

They were people who had families, responsibilities, pleasures and pain. An Indian wife or mother wept with the same bitter tears over a husband or son who had fallen on a battlefield fighting for what they considered right for their people, as the mother of a patriotic soldier of this generation who has given his life for a cause. They were driven by hunger, they became weary in mind and body, and they suffered as a result of disease. They resisted the invasions of the "white man" because they saw devastation as a result of his coming. True, the picture was distorted by evil and greedy white men who exploited their lands, cheated in their bargaining, and abused their women and children, but distorted or not, it produced anger and resentment in the minds of decision makers.

The slaughter of the buffalo by white men for sport and leaving the rotting carcasses on the prairie, did nothing but intensify concern. All the more we should feel pity for the Indian, and shame for those of our society who were at the root of the cause and effect. We should also weep for the many innocents who were caught in the crossfire, and for nothing they had done, suffered the consequences of another's guilt- on both sides of the coin.

It would be well if in the light of our responsibility to evangelize every culture, we put forth the effort to allow to emerge another point of view as it relates to this "alien" people. If for a moment we could observe the Indian culture from within their world, see out of their eyes, and identify with their struggle, perhaps an impartial judgment of their character could justify reason. These were the indigenous Americans.

The early pioneers who penetrated the Indian culture before hatred had induced unfavorable circumstances, wrote something like awe and disbelief about a society that produced no poor, had no neglected orphans, no abandoned widows living a life of loneliness and hunger, and no selfishness in personal dealings. The culture they described was unquestionably more humane than history has given us to believe. If you look at the picture more objectively you will find they were not the filth-ridden, cruel monsters depicted by those who suffered at their hands, but indisputable tenants of a land coveted by others. This would place our focus upon a people who were understanding, yet embittered and disillusioned, fighting for their lands and their emaciated people.

Anyone who was sent to fight against them could testify to the self-discipline and intensity of spirit. They fought ferociously in order to protect what they believed in. They intended to succeed.... or die in the attempt. They were tough and determined. They possessed an endurance that seemed inexhaustible. They lived the best way they could in the environment in which they found themselves, and believed themselves to be victims of cruel men who intended to defraud, divest, and destroy all they held sacred.

It is difficult to say how few "white" scoundrels, who because of personal greed or immoral lust, turned the tide against the peaceable infusion of the past into the future. If the Indian had been understood, it is interesting to contemplate how few wars might have been fought and how different the present would have been.

All information history has passed to us describes a colorful people, deeply religious, and committed to pleasure. There was an exuberance to the American Indian culture, laughter, dress-up, charades, chattering, family and tenderness. The long winter nights were spent by a fireside with "stortellers" that lived and relived the accounts of the past. History was preserved, being passed on from those who knew it best to be programmed into the mind of youth by interesting masters of the trade. One look at the faces of the listener with staring eyes, displayed a mind lost to the present and transported in time by the droning words of the speaker to the actual events of action. Every detail was reduced to simple terminology that fused into the minds of the young.

The echoes of that past now sounds hollow against the haunting after-toll of suffering, of generations left to wallow in tears, relegated to poverty, and living in a destroyed world.

The treaties formulated by the whites were celebrated around gaiety, times of dancing- they were gala affairs. But each treaty was to benefit the future of an advancing people whose mouths watered after the gold that glittered from the Indian's land. A people who gave no thought of the price paid by another if they could achieve their own selfish goals. These treaties were broken many times before the proverbial ink was dry, if circumstances to their being honored was not favorable to the opportunism of those negotiating such a treaty.

In the losing, the American Indian lost more than land. Their vast holdings were parceled, sold, gone. By far the emotional loss was the greatest! They were no longer at home in the land of their ancestors.

During that time when social change was at its greatest intensity, myths were born. Tales of the fur traders, gunmen, cowboys, missionaries and homesteaders filled the pages of historical documents. Only occasionally was there found an Indian in the limelight. From the beginning it seemed that the Indian was to be the dark menace of the myth. Yet there were men of bravery, courage and stamina in every generation of Indian culture. Sadness literally reeks from the shadows as the council chambers echo the voices of many great leaders. "Where are the Pequot?" thundered Tecumseh of the Shawnees, "Where are the Narragansett, the Mohican, the Pokanoket, and many other powerful tribes of our people? They have vanished before the avarice and the oppression of the White Man, as snow before a summer sun.

"Will we let ourselves be destroyed in our turn without a struggle, give up our homes, our country bequeathed to us by the Great Spirit, give up the graves of our dead and everything that is dear and sacred to us? I know you will cry with me, never! Never!"

In 1987, President Ronald Reagan signed a bill into law that designated the route followed by the Cherokee as a historical trail. There was happiness in the minds of the American people that such a thing could be accomplished! But just how far can an act of Congress go to erase the grief caused an entire nation of people?

The story of the Indian is often told from the stages of justification. Their raids upon wagon trains, villages, and homesteaders spoke of cruelty, scalping, and torture. But little is told of the reasons behind such actions. If we could stand still long enough to listen, maybe the events of that sad past could come into focus. Maybe we could at least understand the motive that drove them with such apparent savagery.

In almost every chapter of events that colored the Indian as the aggressor, there were underlying details not known to the mainstream. Stories that will give proper perspective that the Indian was retaliating rather than attacking. Yes, there were Indians that were scoundrels, but in this they were not alone. Every culture has its individuals who become misfits.

Some of the personalities we must blame for the sad series of events during the 19th century were men of position, of prestige, but within were driven by fear of losing a mere political position. There were presidents during that era whose resolve melted before the popular demands of those who pressured for personal gain.

Some of the events of government left John Ross stunned! He was the recognized leader of the Cherokee Nation, and was chosen to represent them in congress. Daniel Webster and other strong principled men stepped to the stage in government to declare copious treaties with phraseology such as

"...they shall be given perpetual ownership....as long as the rivers run and the grass grows." Men of prominence declared such treaties a "base fraud on the Cherokee Indians." To these men the treaties they had signed had provided security for the Indian as a people, and the very government that was established for individual rights, was now seen perpetrating injustice upon an entire culture.

Henry Clay supported with vigor bills that would protect Indian rights. There was hardly a person involved in the conflict who did not recognize that everything that had been done to the Cherokees, and to all Indians, was against everything the United States government was supposed to stand for. For a long time to follow, men in power during those troubled times would suffer pangs of guilt and wonder if there was not something more that could have been done.

Early history was a time spent to develop character and stamina into the lives of the young, to give truth and power for the future. Our present generation was erected upon the traces of those gone before who refused to sacrifice their young. The values this generation has have little room for sacrifice for its youth, if they choose to even allow their birth.

There were many tribes, and customs were as numerous as there were clans. Time and space would not allow for individual descriptions, but I will attempt to expose a few interesting points.

The Apache people were one of the widely known tribes for its fierce retaliation. The Apache basically was a fun-loving, hard-working group of people. They could, however, at a drop of a feather become fierce, brutal, and without mercy. In the everyday activities an adult never struck or harmed a child. The little girls usually could be found at their mother's heels, playing with homemade dolls or learning the fine arts of homemaking and food preparation. The little boys played with bows and arrows, and hunted small game that could be found in the area around their camp. They attended classes held by the warriors and elders of the tribe to learn the art of manhood and warfare. It was said that an Indian child could ride a horse before he could walk.

The Apache Nation was a deeply religious people. Although they recognized numerous denizens of the supernatural world, they did have a supreme deity they called "Ysun or Ussen- The Giver of Life." They believed that it was from this deity that all life generated. They appealed to this spirit for help in coping with everyday problems- drought, illness, and the shortage of game. This power or deity has no sex or place, thus the Apache cannot approach this power directly. The power must work through something and every Apache was a potential recipient. The agent of this power is revealed through dreams and visions, through certain animals and when revealed, becomes the Apache's guardian spirit or his medicine.

Their" God or Life Giver was sometimes called, "Earth Maker," their Madonna was known under a variety of names- "White Painted Woman, White Shell Woman or Changing Woman"; her Son, their Christ, was known as "Child of the Water."

Many things were sacred to the Apache. Turquoise and Abalone Shell are considered to be holy. Each tribe has a sacred mountain that was located near their stronghold. It was upon this mountain that the leaders of the tribe received their visions and dreams they used in guiding their tribe.

The Apache feared death and, even in warfare, took no unnecessary chances in getting themselves killed. When death did strike the family, those who had contact with the dead body had to go through a purification ritual- walking through thick sagebrush smoke and then washing themselves thoroughly in the nearby stream. They had to adorn themselves in new clothing and destroy that which was worn earlier.

The body, along with all his personal possessions, was quickly buried and his wickiup burned to the ground. His name would never again be mentioned by the members of the immediate family or by the tribe.

The purpose of the Apache life was to live a free life. They gradually lost this beloved freedom, but not without a long, exhausting fight. The Spanish Conquistadors were the first to try but soon found they were no match for the spirited, crafty Apache. The Mexican government was the next to try but found the Apache to be elusive for them and they gave up. Finally the United States government got into the act and almost succeeded in ridding the world of the long, feared, dreaded and hated Apaches.

Before being placed on the reservation, the Chiricahua Apache lived a life of freedom and mobility; loved and respected everything the Great Creator had made. They understood and closely related their lives to Mother Earth and the elements of nature- the sky, the sun, moon, stars; the thunder, lightning and rain.

The Chiricahua Apache was equally at home in either the mountains or on the desert. They called Arizona-New Mexico Territory and Old Mexico, especially the northern part, their home. They depended upon nature for their existence and when this was taken from them, they did what any man would do- fight for what was theirs and their father's and their father's father before them.

From the time the Apache first met the White Man, it was nothing but bad news. Their lands and freedom were now in jeopardy and they felt forced to fight for their lands and their right to live their life as they chose. Because of this drastic change, the Apache Nation, particularly the Chiricahua Apaches, became aggressive, restless, brutal, and when they took to the warpath, it was destruction all the way. They raided, plundered and virtually destroyed all who dared to invade their territory. The utterance of the word Apache struck fear into the stoutest, and the fearless.

Slowly the Apache gave up their freedom and the land they loved so very much. The price was high for both sides. Mangas Colorado and Victorio were killed for their beliefs. Geronimo, the last Apache leader to finally give in, kept the Southwest in terror and flame for almost a decade before yielding to his enemy and the reservation. He considered it certain death for he and his followers.

At the height of the Apache warfare, General George Cook decided to try something different in dealing with the Apaches. First, he treated them as human beings and insisted that those under his command do the same. Anyone caught cheating or taking advantage of the Apaches found themselves unemployed. In order to bring law and order to the Apache Nation, General Cook decided to use scouts, made up of none other than Apaches, to hunt out the renegades and bring them to the reservation. When this failed, he used other Apaches as scouts which met with much success. Unknown to General Cook, General Miles and to the Apaches themselves. General Cook's plan would become a tool that the Federal Government would use against the Apaches. Speaking on behalf of the federal government. General Cook promised those who served as Apache scouts would not be harmed when the renegades had been captured and placed, for the last time, on the reservation. When the last of the renegades were placed on the train at Bowie, those faithful men who served as Indian scouts were arrested and placed on the train and headed for Florida. This deceitfulness was long remembered with much bitterness by the scouts and their descendants.

Once they reached Florida, another promise was broken- families were split up, some never again to be reunited. The Chiricahua Apache was unable to adapt themselves to the new climate and environment which resulted in a heavy loss of life. At long last their cries for help and mercy were heard in the hall of Congress and the Chiricahua Apache, what was left of them, were allowed to return to the Southwestern part of the United States, but not to Arizona. Never again would they be allowed to call the Chiricahua Mountains, the Dragoon Mountains, and the Sulfur Springs Valley their home. Instead, they were sent to either the Reservation at Fort Sill, Oklahoma or to the Mescalero Reservation in New Mexico.

The spirit of the long feared Apache Indian was now broken-justice was not, and in many incidences still not, for the Indian.[1]

The church cannot ignore the culture of any people and expect to evangelize them successfully. My feelings are that as long as a cultural value does not clash with biblical principle, there is no danger for the people of that culture to practice those values.

Men seek peace, but the peace they seek so many times is a peace that is molded in the mind of the seeker. As long as the immediate person is not being attacked, then peace can be enjoyed no matter what it has taken to bring about the desired goal. That person can lay aside the events of a past with the changing of a garment, leaving other men to wallow in grief of loss over the same events that have produced tranquillity to the other. This is not so for the church! We are a global community. All of the world's population has the same right to a personal relationship with God, and no one culture should ever try to enclose the gifts of God to the perimeters of culture.

As I previously stated, the Indian mothers that wept in the secret of the teepee over lifeless sons left lying on the battlefield of pioneer days were of the same quality of the mothers who wept in modern homes over sons lost in Vietnam. Sons are the fruit of the womb- life given through a mother's love. Is it possible that the mind dictates reason; a reason that qualifies justification for deeds committed and places one person's reason as right, and another's as wrong, though the reverse may be true?

It is strange that the mind qualifies its own attitudes pertaining to actions that justifies means, or the reasons to reach a desired result. The human mind can imagine right, molded only by what the personal benefits justify.

Since I am speaking about the American Indian in this chapter, I think it is beginning to sift through that there were actions of greedy men- and in some cases- evil men, who charted the course of a great nation at times to provide personal benefit. Presidents and Congress were manipulated into action that had right appearances, but with results that pitted men against men until mothers wept over the needless slaughter of another mother's sons.

For an example, did anyone think of ought but the land before them when the Oklahoma territory was opened? While they waited through the hours previous to the sound of the cannon that announced the race's beginning, did anyone think of the treaties that had given the land "forever" to the Kiowas, the Cheyenne, the Cherokee, and the many other tribes of Indians? Various treaties had given assurances to the Indian as long as the rivers run and the grass grows. Now, with one scratch of the pen upon parchment these treaties were ignored, violated, just as they had been ignored many times before. Just as greed had produced the former loss of the Indian's ancestral homes, once again the advancing tide of land seekers thought only of personal gain. Did anyone see the shine of tears in the eyes of those affected by these events?

However, from the beginning it has been so. Men have abused men!

Footnotes:

[1] Cochise County Historical Society - Betty Orozco

Chapter Fourteen
A HISTORY OF SOME EMERGING MINISTRIES

The Filipino Community

All along the Pacific Rim cities, the Filipino people have emerged as a rapidly growing constituency. With the Filipino enjoying the privileges of immigration ease due the former relationship produced by the Spanish-American War, that number is not expected to decrease.

As the local United Pentecostal Church evangelized its communities, it was only natural that they would tap into this cultural group. One of two national languages spoken by the Filipino people, English, presents no major problem. A beautiful people who find it easy to assimilate into the North American church, they respond to the standards of holiness because they are a clean, moral people who love that part of the church's message

From a local church sponsoring a Filipino conference, there was a response from the total west coast, extending from San Diego, California, to Seattle, Washington. Again, it was only natural that Multicultural Ministries would be engaged, and as a result the pastors of these constituents requested that a conference of greater dimension be created. During the gathering of the Filipinos in Seattle, Washington, the organization of this activity was turned over to the General Home Missions Division.

The First Annual Filipino Evangelism Conference was convened in San Diego, California in June of 1994. Nearly ten thousand dollars was pledged by the attendees to further evangelism among the Filipino residing in North America, and Multicultural Ministries became dedicated to extend the gospel to this cultural group.

A task force committee was formed and chaired by Benny Patayan, Jr., son of the national secretary of the United Pentecostal Church of the Philippine Islands. This committee has accepted the responsibility of reaching all of North America with the precious truth of the gospel.

Montreal, Canada, was impacted. With a local base of several Filipino families, it was a natural that the east coast would also respond to Multicultural Ministries' evangelism program to the Filipino. Ricardo Zabala, pastoring a Filipino congregation in Calgary, Alberta, Canada, was the invited minister for this gathering jointly sponsored by the Montreal church and its pastor, Paul Graham, and Multicultural Ministries.

Don Hanscom, a returned missionary, having served in Pakistan, was appointed to be the assistant coordinator of Multicultural Ministries during the 1994 General Conference convening in Milwaukee, Wisconsin. With the growing responsibilities of this ministry, and the vital part it was playing in world-evangelism, the church needed a secure leadership.

The French

While no adequate census report has produced a total number of French speaking population in North America, a study of the U.S. Census Bureau shows that in the United States, Maine has the highest population of French speakers per capita, followed by Louisiana. New Hampshire and Vermont also use French as a second language. In general, the French culture residing in North America is the third most widely used language after dominant English and second place Spanish. Alabama, Arkansas, D.C., Florida, Georgia, Maryland, Mississippi, South Carolina, Tennessee, Virginia, and West Virginia use French as a third language. My investigation resulted in a breakdown for Canada through 1990: As of 1992, Canada has a land area of 9,976,140 square kilometers (3,851,809 square miles), and a total population of 27,352.000. This provides a population density of 7.1 persons per square mile. 80% of Canada's population is concentrated within 160 km (86 miles) of its Southern border with the United States. 77.5% live in cities such as Montreal, Toronto and Vancouver, and 22.5% in rural areas; 8,097,480 are French; 385,375 are Indians called 1st Nation Residents, and 31,085 Eskimos. Over 5 million French communicate in the French language.

The population growth of Canada over the last decade was .78%. 21% of the population is under the age of 15, with only 11.3% over the age of 65, making Canada a ripe spiritual harvest field.

As I saw the pressing need to reach the French speaking people of North America, I suggested that the General Home Missions Division create a viable program of evangelism that would concentrate upon the hot-bed of North America's largest French population- Quebec, Canada! With a policy structure much as we have for the other ministries operating under Multicultural Ministries, it would leave the administration of the French under the control of each district in which the ministry is located. A five year goal would also be submitted in order to keep an assessment of successes.

I believed, and it proved to be true, that the most productive efforts would take place in Quebec and New Brunswick, Canada, and the states of Maine, New Hampshire and Vermont would react on the periphery. Louisiana's Cajun French would then catch the vision, spilling over into the Creole French of South Florida.

As a result, Brother Cunningham sent me to New Brunswick to meet with a representation of French speaking pastors and leaders. They were impacted to learn that the GHMD was considering opening a Multicultural Ministries activity that would include the French. Tentatively, we organized a task force committee for the planning of activities, and to act as an energizing agent for the French culture. Brother Goddard, as a

Regional Director for the GHMD, accepted the responsibility to serve on the committee. As we later learned, he was a positive influence that greatly enhanced the program. As the New Brunswick District Home Missions Director, his participation was a vital part to the success of the endeavor.

I was a firm believer that the members of the committee should be made up of either French cultural participants, or men who have a good success record with French evangelism. We selected Gilles Essiambre, Paul Graham, John Thevenot and Willis Arbeau to represent Canada's vast French population, and Jonathan Suber, from Louisiana to represent the states on the committee. The plans as I laid them out to the Home Missions Executive Committee, were approved and ratified. The ball was in the court of Multicultural Ministries.

Our next step was to pound out a policy that would be acceptable to the New Brunswick District, and be broad enough to serve the continuity of the emerging French Evangelism Ministries. The purpose, structure and goals would be in keeping with the present policy governing other minority language groups, but it would be modified to make it unique to the French speaking culture.

The purpose simply stated that French Evangelism Ministries would be established to evangelize the French culture residing in North America, and to provide fellowship for the French speaking believers of the United Pentecostal Church. Further purpose would be defined as assisting in the development and licensing of French leaders, creating and planning an annual French conference of evangelism, and produce evangelism and training materials in the French cultural languages

French Evangelism Ministries was designed, as in the other ministries, to function under the auspices of The General Home Missions Division, and be responsible to the Coordinator of Multicultural Ministries. The committee consisted of a chairman, a secretary, and four delegates. The task force committee was asked to serve as the first official members of the committee.

Brother Goddard and I met with the New Brunswick District Board to present our plan, along with a proposal to bring the First Annual French Evangelism Conference to Montreal. It met with resounding approval! The board was not only pleased, but offered every assistance to make the conference a success.

The actual conference was scheduled for June 23 - 24, 1994. From the very first evening, God placed His hand of approval upon the proceedings, and miraculous results were obvious. The sanctuary was packed by the last evening until standing room only was available. Ministers from Maine, Louisiana, and Mississippi were in attendance, as were ministers seeking the will of God for their lives. The services were in French with the exception of where the speakers were English. These were translated simultaneously from the pulpit to French. French Evangelism Ministries was a success from the very first activity!

With the new policy approved and in effect, every district official can ascertain that the administration is totally under his control, and that Multicultural Ministries will assist in evangelism, but the solving of situations is to be kept strictly under the control of the district, and the section in which any situation should arise.

With the experiences gleaned from the many activities Multicultural Ministries is involved in, it stands to offer suggestions and assistance as the church incorporates minority groups into the evangelism programs of the United Pentecostal Church.

Chapter Fifteen
The Need Of A Cultural Bridge

The administration of multicultural groups within the United Pentecostal Church International is a very important priority for the leadership. Indispensable to a tranquil assimilation by minority language groups into the policies and programs of sectional and district activities is a reporting system that gives precise information for those who are in elective positions, while continuing to leave an open-ended avenue of evangelism for the cultural group. Assimilation is an important factor.

We speak of assimilation for those who come to us from other cultures, but what we mean is that they assimilate into the structure of the established administration, and acquire a knowledgeable understanding of how the system operates, the adherence to the Articles of Faith, and that the assimilating believe and practice the doctrine of the church. Furthermore that emerging ministers from among our multicultural groups understand and comply with the various ministerial requirements. We are not necessarily talking about assimilation in the secular sense.

Since culture is a very emotional issue, the presence of a coordinator, whether it be on the district or the national level, is a positive move in the right direction. On the reporting issue, he will interpret communication. This is at times very critical. Where cultural ambiguity would give the leadership unnecessary concerns, a coordinator can fine-tune requests, underline needs, and insure a tranquil communication, whereas the absence of such a mediator can lead to misunderstandings that could cause irreparable damage.

Furthermore, Multicultural Ministries calls for more of a hands-on style of leadership due the speed of change that must be undergone. Many cultural groups now entering into a relationship with the United Pentecostal Church International not only come from all points of the globe, but from a wide spectrum of political systems. Those who migrate from dictatorial styles of government have never experienced the liberties of thinking out answers for themselves, nor have they enjoyed the privilege of speaking out on issues. For these brand new areas of activity, they will need someone who can settle anxiety, sort out the frustration, and guarantee that they will develop properly within the system. Because these speedy changes are so rapid for many multicultural groups, a mediator, whom we call a coordinator, should act as a bridge and keep the pace of development steady.

The administration has neither the time, nor the budget to have the many meetings necessary to work out rudimentary issues important to the assimilation process. Therefore, there must be a high degree of delegation in the area of coordination. There is the need of development for new converts, and the installation of evangelism strategy. The coordinator is able to provide the hands-on relationship for these activities while the administration retains the control of the governmental structure. Since the coordinator operates within the system and under the direction of administration, the safeguards are in place to insure harmony. The coordinator acts as a bridge to, and from, our variegated Ethnic cultures.

Heightened sensitivity in these areas is vital to the success of Multicultural Ministries. The coordinator, while very important to new dimensions of positive direction, must be of impeccable ethics. He cannot develop a following from among the constituency, nor create even a remote style of administration. He must remember that he is a coordinator for evangelism, and must divorce himself from any administrative action. His role is to be an ambassador of culture for the administration in that he does not make decisions that will effect those in the leadership. He cannot speak in a manner in which he, himself, views an issue. He must represent the administration, and interpret for those whom he serves, the views and desires of that administration. If he cannot truthfully, and honestly, commit himself to the rule of this ethic, he should withdraw himself from his position. He does not create rules; he works harmoniously with them, and compassionately leads others to do the same.

In order to clarify the church's position, let's take the message a step farther. The church community must develop a deep reverence for the sacredness of a person's culture, and our inter-connectedness. There are the people the Lord has commissioned us to evangelize, and we have a definite responsibility toward them. Therefore, our quest to reach them with the gospel will entail emerging mutual appreciation. Somewhere we must judge righteously about issues that have their origin in culture. However, these are not issues for the coordinator to decide. He has no power to neither dictate nor judge in matters that pertain to the administration. His position is one of representation.

In the coordinator, what we see is a person who is quietly going about making a big difference. The less we note about his activity, the greater his results. He is merely guiding those for whom he is coordinating to distinctive mental destinations, and assisting to obtain objectives desired by the administration. We are spending an inordinate amount of time as a church trying to do things well, and in areas where the delegation of responsibility could alleviate many hours of concern for those who have matters of greater importance to attend to. It would be a wise decision to delegate such responsibility. Probably the most wasteful hours, and the most frustrating, are those spent trying to do something well which you shouldn't be doing at all. I firmly believe even with the best intentions, members of administration should not involve themselves in cultural ambiguity. There are simply too many ramifications. Why not apply those hours of effort and frustration in other areas, and allow a coordinator to work out all the details and present positive documentation translated to inform the leadership. Judgment can then be made without the pressure of the imperceptible mental factors that accompany cultural situations.

I believe the United Pentecostal Church International is beginning to sense the important role it is playing in world evangelism. We have made great advances toward the goals of "The Whole Gospel To The Whole Word", and we will continue to extend the boundaries of His kingdom. But as in many areas of professional strategy, we need special emphasis and focus to realize our goals. As the church takes a good look at evangelism, internal and external strengths can be harnessed to assist in accessing greater potentials. We must be willing to make our evangelism strategies flexible, plan for contingencies, and take a good look at administration structure to include changes that will favor evangelism goals.

There is no one right way to evangelize the whole world. But the lessons we are learning need to be well employed to remain as important resources for the future. In other words, we need not repeat the mistakes of the past. Innovation will provide opportunity and tremendous growth potential as we incorporate new ideas and acceptable flexibility in evangelism, while administration continues to carry the legal responsibilities it was designed to perform, and in the manner in which policy dictates its principles.

On the domestic front we are penetrating deeply into the same cultures our foreign missionaries are commissioned to evangelize. There must be a common factor at work to unite the overall effort in order to retain the momentum we have initiated. The answer is simple. A national coordinator can sift potential problems from the sandstorm effect, and inform the leadership of both the positives and the negatives involved in multicultural evangelism and missionary efforts world-wide.

Therefore the coordinator must work within the structure guaranteeing that every step forward be made with a resolution that what he is doing is greater than he... bigger than his ambition and dreams.... bigger than his perspective. He must believe that what he is doing is right, and create a mentality that his commitment is to serve his administration. That mentality will translate to his attitude and consequently to those he represents. In as much as he is the person with understanding of both sides of the cultural question, he will be the person to communicate awareness and information about multicultural problems and their possible solutions. In this he will be a valuable asset to the administration.

The Coordinator And Awareness

The coordinator will strive to awaken the awareness of those involved in evangelism. He will coordinate the evangelism process by weaving the results into the policies and programs of the administration. Awareness precedes action. No one will get excited about evangelizing our Ethnic communities until it can be proven that they will make a big difference, and that the difference will relate in a positive manner to their local congregation. New programs must constantly be created that will transcend the cultural barriers that exist as obstacles to evangelism. Again, it is the coordinator that will dedicate himself to this important task. He must remain up to date with statistics and immigration changes. His files will become gorged with information about where distinctive cultures are congesting society, and he will coordinate members of the spiritual family as they physically move from one area of the world to another. On the district front his steps will be directed to the inner-city structure where communities of the same culture converge, and becoming a common friendly visitor, he will not only create avenues of trust, but an influence that will bond even the most elusive person to his cause.

Our ongoing successes in the world arena will depend upon the fact that he will constantly be called upon to make productive changes. If we want to change the world, then we must first change ourselves. We must think globally, but act locally. Our changes must first take place in the heart and radiate to attitude. The coordinator by virtue of his knowledge of culture can be one who could communicate where changes will effect us in a positive manner, and where detrimental changes will reduce our effectiveness. His communication about change will be retained in the area of administration, and will never violate the administration's position until proper approvals for variations have had decisive action.

There is a beauty in diversity. No where is the love of God more beautifully displayed, and evangelism more productive, than in a congregation where all of God's creation is worshipping together, and where cultural lines are transcended with acceptance. Diversity in a congregation speaks to a community that prejudice is unacceptable, and that "whosoever will" really means what it says in the language of the soul winner. Again, the coordinator in an effective manner can influence congregations who are situated in a community of Ethnic diversity, to infuse the constituents of that community into the church, and assist both the dominant and the minority culture in the assimilation process.

It would be very foolish indeed to imagine that by bringing in a diversity of cultural entities, we will not have difficulty. Trouble can arise when complexities are introduced. But because the church is in the people business, and people is its only business, it will face up to these problems by having candid discussions about what we are up against, and through proper adjustments turn the negatives into positives. The proper solution to cultural problems is to confront the issue with a willingness to change, if that change will give us a more productive direction.

Conflict is not only normal, but necessary for certain kinds of development in the spiritual arena. It is in conflict we define ourselves. Difficulties will prevail only when the church avoids conflict and allows it to fester. A successful coordinator will keep the administration aware of opportunities for conflict resolution and policy making, and soon former barriers to harmonious interaction will have disappeared. As education and understanding remove ambiguities, the church builds confidence and shares visions of evangelism with other congregations fearful to initiate steps into similar fields of harvest.

Churches that have created diversity within the congregation have experienced such positive results, they would never return to their former status. It has been said by many that it was one of the best decisions they have ever made. It all boils down to the philosophy and ability to understand other cultures, and deal with the differences. A Multicultural Ministries coordinator will be invaluable to a local church experiencing the growth pains due cross-culture evangelism.

The challenges of cultural ambiguity are among the greatest a church faces. Because of this, many churches are busy developing harmony strategies that will be accessed when the need arises. It is always better to have a policy and never need it, than to experience the need of a non-existent rule of action. Therefore a word to the wise would be that church policy include the contingencies that may develop.

A pastor whose life has been devoted to evangelism, will always consider alternative productive methods of growth. He divests himself of ego during times of crisis and opportunity. He calls upon those who can best direct him to proper avenues of choice, and proceeds to action. Here again, without creating a following among the constituents of a local congregation, the Multicultural Ministries coordinator is available. With valuable advice and counsel, he can create new life for the church needing help in assimilating multicultural constituents. In all actuality, a new future is possible for a church that will cross formidable, but productive cultural lines to reach magnificent fields of harvest.

The choices are many, but they require taking time to investigate proper courses to pursue. Decisions must be firmly made, for a hasty choice to enter multicultural evangelism can destroy both desire and purpose if the guidelines of a harmonious assimilation for the converts are not established. A church congregation must understand the transformation that will inevitably effect the church. Priorities must be sorted out and tolerance buffers anticipated.

Paradoxically, Multicultural Ministries coordinators must lead while always denying themselves a position of authority. They become a part of the stairwell by which new dimensions are experienced by the congregation, but knowingly remain an indistinct part of the growth, ready to fade into obscurity when no longer needed. They infuse stability for a congregation by providing openness and foundation for beginning, but will be the scaffolding that will be removed and stacked as no longer needed after the structure begins to function.

For the church, ambivalence is often fierce and extends throughout the spiritual family, as members protest cultural influences that invariably produce change in ordinary customs. However, importantly, this is seen as a necessary condition for change, not its impediment. Most generally, the congregation secretly admires the growth pattern the church has developed, even though sometimes the sacrifice of some personal values are felt keenly. It is merely a matter of what is good and what is better on the scales of evangelism results.

As greater efforts are put in place to evangelize our Ethnic cultures, the church will face issues never before experienced. The pastor's position undergoes emotional challenges. His duel roles of chief executive and shepherd complicates decision making as he brings into balance many delicate matters that will at time confuse a local congregation. As chief executive of the church, he must insure the congregation they will not be forgotten as important decisions seem to favor the minority culture. The pastor having insured himself of the will of God, wisely fuses the cultural entities of the church into a living relationship of brotherhood, and communicates satisfaction that the congregation is fulfilling the commission to reach its community. These measures properly instituted, and fairly imposed, will spark new life into any church body.

However, please allow me to express without a desire to compromise our articles of faith, that we must view ourselves- and allow the world to view us- as a wonderfully conservative unique body of believers with the good points and the bad points that word connotes and implies. We in the United Pentecostal Church have many points of personal choice that provide a very limited and confining view of ourselves. Somehow we must come to a place where we can see that the world we were commissioned to evangelize is bigger than we are. That many of our cultural guidelines are not necessarily biblical principles and hinders the growth factor. We as human, and therefore with an ambivalent nature, cannot set guidelines of godliness that emanate out of a cultural perspective. We must continue to practice a biblical standard that can transcend every racial and cultural barrier with an identical and righteous judgment of what is God ordained. When we can accomplish this surgical procedure upon ourselves and our mentality, we will step to the cutting edge of revival among the minority groups who populate our continent.

Chapter Sixteen
Evangelism, Revival, And Multicultural Ministries

The preceding chapters are important to the education of those interested in cross-cultural evangelism. They provide the basic information that motivates the urgency of a new dimension in evangelism for the local church. The innovative pastor can see that Multicultural Ministries is very effectively bringing to birth a revival of consequence in the United Pentecostal Church. In the fading light of the evening time, representatives of the world's cultural cross-section are coming to the proximity of North American pulpits. Since end-time revival increasingly involves our ethnic cultures, we must step forward to accept our responsibility to lead the world from the dark chaos of spiritual uncertainty, and bring it to the dawning of a new day. Each of us must persevere to adequately equate the value of emotional struggle and calculate answers, not only for ourselves, but for those who depend upon our leadership. In the light of world evangelism we can be assured that our cause is just, and our objective is right. If there should be future generations that follow us, let them understand that we properly assessed the need, opened the doors to our hearts and to our churches, and brought about the final assimilation of the world's cultures into the church. Let them be able to say that we stood where commitment to the commission required us to stand.

What is at stake in Multicultural Ministries is more than a few struggling ethnic peoples; it is a brand new beginning for the church where diverse cultures are drawn together to fulfill the desires of God to reach His world. It is to achieve the universal aspirations of mankind: to find peace among peers in a house of worship without prejudice, and to know the fullness of truth. Such a world is worthy of our struggle.

We can look back on great achievements. We have resisted appeasement and risen by desire to conquer cynicism for our accomplishments, both within us and outside us, and paved the road for this great revival to reach our doors. We have accepted the world in the spirit of our Master, loving it while reaching for it, embracing it to our bosom without unacceptable demands upon cultural differences. The blending of cultures in the United Pentecostal Church International is a victory for everyone in that we have removed the emotional barriers that Satan had erected as a final deterrent of the church.

The principle that has guided us during this process is simple: our objective was to help struggling humanity to encounter God while establishing unchanging doctrinal expectations. And in this we did not exclude anyone!

As Multicultural Ministry develops, procedure and policy will be carefully analyzed. Let it be known that it is the desire of our multicultural constituency to fulfill biblical responsibilities as they accept the benefits of this fellowship. As a reward for acceptance, they will broadcast the message to the far extremities of the world; the world the United Pentecostal Church has a genuine burden to reach. The message of salvation will be conveyed by powerful messengers who can penetrate both cultural and social barriers, achieving by natural birth what others of us are merely trained to accomplish. By the same principle contact with new immigrants coming to these shores from any country will be made. Multicultural Ministries will be involved in seeking and saving, not qualifying and accepting. We will encourage continued commitment to evangelism, and maintain a distance from administration. In this manner our established presbyter system will operate without encumbering hindrance and disorganization.

For 50 years the UPCI has served the world as an inspiring example of the Christian faith. It has led the struggle for lost humanity everywhere. Our people have financed the outreaches of world evangelism until the "sun never sets upon the endeavors of the United Pentecostal Church". We certainly will not fail to meet the challenge merely because the stage has been transferred from the field abroad to the domestic front. We realize there will be sacrifice of personal ideas and the crossing of formidable racial barriers with cataclysmic changes. Those changes will many times shake our dominant cultural values. But it is HIS world, and HIS message, that we must keep before us. We are United Pentecostals and we have the unique responsibility to do the work of evangelism, not perpetuate a system.

Together, we are resolute and resourceful. Together, we have unselfishly sacrificed our means for the sake of the gospel in lands far away. Now together, surely, we can create an atmosphere of giving to reach those of the same foreign cultures who inhabit this land wherein we dwell. The results of our giving will indeed initiate a continual redundancy as the gospel grips new personnel with the burden to reach their own. As evangelism swells to the crescendo of lengthening shadows, our investments will have produced greater returns.

While the problems before us may be different, the key to solving those problems remains the same. It boils down to the individual who will remove opposition and allow free access to the fountains of life, no matter the face of the thirsty.

Culture Is Important

Culture is a commanding factor in dealing with evangelism. As this book has outlined, we will be successful in our mission to present the gospel to other cultures outside our own when we take into consideration the values of those cultures.

The problems pertaining to cross-culture evangelism are not a modern development. They have plagued the church from the very beginning. Men have found that even as Christians they have been controlled by the dictates of culture and felt impelled to pass them on as scriptural concepts. However, we must not limit God, who is the Lord of all, to the confining limitations of culture.

Unless the church is prepared to look beyond the boundaries of the culture in which it exists, our goal of evangelizing the entire world will be hindered. The early church fathers recognized this problem and stepped to the front to eliminate it. Even the emotional appeal of the Apostle James as he dictates changes that affected the local church relative to circumcision were received as necessary by those involved in evangelism.

I do not intend to imply, nor do I advocate, that we should ever compromise biblical truth. We must adhere to those things the Bible teaches regardless of cultural differences. But at the same time, we must not oppose cultural values simply because they differ from our own.

In the secular world there is often a negative reaction to the many ethnic cultures that are ever increasing in the United States and Canada. However, for those who hold world evangelism as a priority, something beautiful is coming into focus that could drastically change concepts we have held over the years.

With this thought in mind, I present an emotional and factual challenge in the hope that I can contribute something toward new strategies that will enhance our results. We must preach Christ to a lost and dying world, and we all agree that we need adjustments in order to succeed in the face of world population growth and spiritual opposition.

The world we are to evangelize is divided into many diverse language and cultural groups. Since representatives of those groups are coming to the United States and Canada in astounding numbers, the United Pentecostal Church International has an unparalleled opportunity in world evangelism, as well as an unparalleled responsibility.

One billion people comprise the Chinese language and culture group. In other words, one out of five persons living on the earth is Chinese. The world's third largest language group is Spanish. Sandwiched between is the English-speaking populace, of whom we are a part. Without the mediation of expertise in language and culture, what hope is there that we can effectively reach the Chinese world? Or, how can we reach the Spanish of Latin America and Spain, along with a multitude of other language and cultural groups that abound on the earth? That is what this book has addressed. The sun is rising upon the church's greatest opportunity ever to reach the entire world from the pulpits of North America. We must rise and take the initiative into willing hands to adjust whatever activity necessary to apprehend that opportunity. A few attitudes we have guarded only too well must be sacrificed upon the altar of evangelism.

The concept of sending missionaries to reach the world will be enhanced as we evangelize the many variegated cultures abounding on this continent. We can develop and train the converts who result from our efforts and through them, reach their world! Once we realize that God is in control of the process, global conquest as it relates to world evangelism can be realized.

God is arranging the world's future by bringing key figures of tomorrow's church in contact with the gospel today! God controls the moves of people who make history, and it is in this light that the increasing numbers of ethnic cultures residing in the United States and Canada should be viewed. What is happening is God's doing, and ripe golden grain is arriving to the proximity of the garners. It is our responsibility as church leaders to recognize- and accept- the changing face of North America as a fertilizing agent of evangelism, and move forward with a confidence that we are a part of great things looming on the imminent horizon.

There is a miniature world residing within the boundaries of the United States and Canada. This world is multiplying daily as people from the third world realize their dreams of coming to this continent. They come from everywhere, give every kind of reason, and go beyond limits of our understanding to succeed in their purpose. They simply want to become Americans.

Fleeing all manner of pressure from political upheaval and economic disaster to religious persecution, those who succeed in coming into the atmosphere of freedom- even those illegal in status- do so with hearts filled with gratitude. Most of them are legal, and those who are not usually do not consider that they have transgressed a law. Many have suffered violent displacement because of civil war. Their countries have been devastated and laid waste. Often they are victims of hatred and vengeance from people of opposing political or religious views; many times even from family members. The most desperate make their way across deserts, seas, and rivers, braving all kinds of dangers, to flee poverty, oppression, and despair in search of a better life.

Thus to these shores come the immigrant. Typically he stands at loss for linguistic understanding, having little or no knowledge of the culture in the land to which he has come. All he knows is, here is refuge! In this spirit, people come from all over the world by the millions and determine that come what may, here they will stay.

As a general rule, people of all cultures who immigrate to this country, do so with the intention of becoming loyal, patriotic, flag-waving citizens of their newly adopted country. And each in time blends into the North

American culture with varying degrees of success.

The Mexican who arrives here and cross an invisible line does not feel the same dislocation that other immigrants know. Mexico and the United States blend into one another almost as continuously as the sky that covers them. It is the only place in the world where someone can jump from the third world to the first world in five minutes. In spite of all border precautions, arrival is made easy by an inexpensive plane ride, or even by foot across the Mexican border.

Immigrants to the United States tend to live together in selected areas where a greater security can be felt. But the trend seems stronger, or at least more visible, among the Hispanics and the Asians. For one thing, their sheer numbers enable them to congregate in more sizable groups than previous waves of immigrants could. Perhaps more importantly, as they come today in increasing numbers, they find a greater strength.

As much as North America is a mosaic of cultures, it is amazing that barriers exist. One of the greatest challenges of the church is to remove those barriers and constructively erect a platform upon which to build an effective fellowship. How much of a barrier there is depends upon individual churches and how they view the people of their communities.

Proclaiming the beautiful gospel message to a proud race of people who have different tastes and customs- not to speak of the language and understanding barrier- is a formidable responsibility. Yet, while difficult, we must never think of the task as impossible.

Our efforts are made less demanding by the fact we are propagating a message that is indispensable. Moreover, immigrating people tend to trust American people in general, and even more so, those of the church. Then too, the gospel itself has an enormous power upon the lives of people. Important also is the knowledge that God will blend all people of all cultures and language into one body called the church.

When we understand the scope of God's plan in bringing the wheat to the proximity of the garner, we will see opportunities for the church that we never dreamed possible. If we can learn to love and understand the cultural groups residing in our neighborhoods, we will be able to evangelize them, train them, and allow the church to send them to many areas of the world heretofore closed to us. Prepared by culture and language at natural birth, and commissioned and sent by spiritual rebirth, these ready-made missionaries can spread the gospel to the far ends of the world. We will see a global impact by our perseverance in this matter. Through spiritual birth, we all become one people, with one purpose-to evangelize the world before Jesus comes.

As an example let us think of the possibility of going behind the Bamboo Curtain! Evangelizing the Chinese of America could produce a missionary of consequence. There are in excess of one billion Chinese divided into nine major language dialects. Mandarin holds the top spot with 552 million, Wu is spoken by 76 million, Cantonese by 60 million, and Taiwanese by 13 million. The dream goes on.

English dominates the second place in language grouping with some 500 million native speakers. Then comes the Spanish language with a constituency in excess of 300 million. When we see the possibilities of what God could accomplish by the gathering of these language groups into the proximity of the North American church, we can only stand with head bowed.

It is important to have an understanding of a person's culture when seeking to win him to the gospel. When we comprehend the social structure of a particular segment of our world, we will know how churches are likely to be established and propagated through it and what action will tend to destroy those opportunities. An understanding of people and their culture greatly influences when, how, and to what extent the gospel will flow through that segment of society.

Most Hindu, Buddhists, Confucianists, and Moslems resist the Christian faith. Often they do so, not out of theological considerations, but out of fear that becoming a Christian will separate them from their own people. The great obstacle to conversion is social, not theological.

A great turning to Christ- even the end-time revival we desire- will happen if we can blend our efforts to accept the responsibility of understanding and reaching our ethnic cultures. Ethnic loyalty exerts a profound influence, both for and against evangelistic endeavors. We must learn to use it to the advantage of the gospel. We must work within the existing cultures, not attempt to establish a new one.

As the church faces the task of evangelizing the world, it is racing the rapture! There has never been a time when a greater effort for world-missions was more needed. We need programs that fall in step with apostolic methods. It is not that we have not enjoyed great results with past programs, nor that great men have not labored through the midday sun, but we must face up to the truth that unless God intervenes and helps us with innovative dynamics, millions will remain unreached.

We must not focus merely upon short term achievements- no matter how dramatic- but upon calculated results that will provide solid stages of development. We cannot build upon ambivalent human values or ideology, but upon God's eternal purpose. Our personal involvement must become only threads woven into the fabric of God's will.

The reason behind the church's very existence is to save the world. We are to reach every creature in every part of God's world! We are the mechanism that reaches into every culture and language to bring light to those bathed in darkness. We have a responsibility to a message of salvation that replaces chaos and disorder.

When we reach out and take the initiative into new and exciting areas, when we can adjust to changing times while holding fast to unchanging values, we will overcome obstacles on the periphery. We must constantly apply pressure to mold our present into an acceptable future. If we delay in seasons of harvest, we will see dreams die and visions fade.

Evangelizing the world and bringing converts into a living faith in Christ must somehow be the consuming effort of our constituency. This commitment must create such a burden that priorities will center on evangelism. Our missionaries, both at home and abroad, must be supported as an extension of ourselves, for they have gone in our stead. We must do everything possible to reach the lost, not only those of our kind, but those of other cultures, colors, and languages. With this in mind, an astronomical task becomes an astronomical opportunity! As some of our greatest preachers have preached, "The power behind us is greater than the task before us!"

World evangelism in anyone's vocabulary begins with home missions. There is no foreign missionary until someone at home is evangelized. No one could go- properly underwritten- without the support of friends in the local church at home. Even a growing, productive foreign field would stagger if there were not growing numbers of new churches on the home front to increase financial giving.

That is why we must turn the floodlights on the increasing numbers of ethnic people converging onto North American soil. Do we of the church have a rising secular feeling of concern and distain, or do we view them as an opportunity to evangelize? Do we believe God to be in control?

God has transformed North America into a nation of nations. Every conceivable culture of the world has immigrated to the back doors of our churches. This situation enables North American pulpits to overcome culture barriers with cross-culture evangelism. Every North American United Pentecostal can now become a missionary to foreign lands without leaving the perimeter of his neighborhood. Joining forces with Canada, the United States accepts the challenge to evangelize this strange and complex mosaic of cultures.

There is no time for analyzing or lamenting the past. Everyone agrees that the United Pentecostal Church has greatly expended itself. Without considering the impossibilities of our task we need to do everything within our power to accomplish the growing responsibility of our mission, leaving the impossibilities to the God who gave the mandate.

Propagation of the gospel begins with language and culture. A multitude of societies make up our world, and essential to evangelizing each society is an understanding of its social structure. No one understands cultural specifics as well as someone born into that society. For that reason, if we will focus attention upon the multicultural population within the reach of our North American pulpits, we will greatly benefit world evangelism.

With the information we have gleaned and experiences we have incorporated into the system, it is apparent that English-speaking pastors with a burden and love for people can effectively evangelize and disciple people of other languages and culture. Moreover, if we will involve ourselves in cross-cultural evangelism with a purpose, we will not only bulge the seams of our churches, but we may set into motion the very principle needed to reach the world before Jesus returns. Let us lift up our eyes and see the light over the horizon of our responsibility and opportunity.

Can we of this day, with an intentional effort, give our minds some new longitude and latitude to adjust our evangelistic efforts? Can it be possible that with these adjustments we can increase the potential of reaching our world? That is the question posed to the United Pentecostal Church, and it demands an answer.

The need to develop proper church growth patterns among our ethnic-American cultures is a formidable one. Differences in lifestyles require that priorities and programs be established carefully and within the accepted guidelines of those districts most affected by the results.

Sometimes there are no uniform answers, but a successful program will resolve conflicts, establish priorities, and set the course for future problem solving. It is important that we move with caution, lest wrong moves cause us to miss important principles that would provide permanent success patterns.

Multicultural Ministries, as it has been structured by the General Home Missions Division of the United Pentecostal Church has been very successful to this point. While I prefer that our successes continue to judge merit, I think we have laid a great deal of the groundwork necessary to pursue an effective course in cross-culture evangelism. However, to go beyond recommendation and counsel, and to begin implementing a permanent program, we need leadership, dedication, and a broad base of support from all sectors.

What we have produced in Multicultural Ministries is an awareness of the possibilities! Multicultural Ministries has reflected an image of the future- an imperfect image, no doubt- but one that best represents today's estimate of tomorrow's goals. We must remember that the assumptions upon which these activities are based will change with time as more permanent and mature programs emerge.

To accept the responsibilities of implementation and face the problems that are attached to those possibilities, we must also accept the responsibility to modify the program with patience until we have a workable and uniform principle successfully operating throughout all of North America. It is imperative, in view of the needs forcing themselves upon us, to continue to establish a long range program.

Yes, the task ahead is complex! The challenge is difficult and at times worrisome. However, the future is dependent upon how vigorously we meet that challenge. The future will not wait upon us to decide, it will be molded by those who will persevere by necessity.

Recent times have produced a deep love for the ethnic cultures who have been fused into the constituency of the United Pentecostal Church International. Understanding cultural differences has resulted in a compassion among many of our pastors who are now more capable of distinguishing cultural idiosyncrasies from biblical transgression. Time has also produced a knowledge of the substantial opportunities that wait to be apprehended regarding Spanish and other ethnic language ministries. Now is the time to rise and accept the challenge with thanksgiving, and write history for our sons and daughters to read. I know of no greater era in which so much depended upon the outreach abilities of the United Pentecostal Church International!

Chapter Seventeen
The Jesus Method

This book is about evangelism. I am writing in the early hours before dawn and peering through tears as I concentrate upon the purpose for which I write. I want to be a blessing to my generation, and leave the marks of my passing etched upon my peers. I have not written to cast blame, but to find appropriate answers for the task of evangelism. All who have been associated with me during the years of my ministry will attest to the fact that I have lived to serve my church and my community.

To prepare the local pastors for the arduous task of evangelizing the ethnic people of North America, I have made a new study into the life of Jesus Christ. I felt that in studying His method perhaps we could better understand the dynamics of evangelism. There is no adequate way to describe the ministry of Jesus in the terms of our modern day vernacular and give it justice. However, pouring over the record, there seems to be a pattern that emerges out of His actions. That His ministry deeply touched the human heart we can agree, because our hearts are tremendously moved merely by reading the account. From the manner in which He came into the world, taking on the nature of the people he came to reconcile to His death on Calvary, there was a total surrender to the purpose for which He had come. This we understand, but to put into practice those same simple principles we have learned about Him (using the balance of human reasoning), I fear we would find it next to impossible.

As I contemplated the ministry of Christ at other times, many of the characteristics of His ministry were overlooked. During those beautiful hours of study I was so tuned to His person, I missed His method.

Our Lord's message to mankind lost no time dealing with the negative side of humanity, but quickly brought the focus upon the positive. The worth of a soul... the temporal as connected to the body, and the eternal characterized by the soul... Seeking first the Kingdom of God and His righteousness, then devoting efforts to enrich the conveniences of life... These were His tactics. His total ministry was an optimistic approach toward suffering, trial, and sacrifice. He taught that all of these things were common to mankind, but could be permanently altered by a purposeful preparation for eternal rewards.

Jesus had a unique ability that was constantly present in his preaching. He denounced sin, but He loved the sinner. Kindness toward the oppressed, but a harsh reprimand toward those who made unreasonable demands. His message and His actions were synonymous. We have the Bible's account of his life on earth, but we must study with intent to understand the method of his ministry. His words had such impact upon the people that He drew "multitudes" into desert places, remote mountainsides, seashores, and as His fame went out, the scriptures emphasize that "the whole city" went out to hear Him. In short, He "reached" the people!

Jesus was successful in His purpose because He communicated with the inner longings of people. He used the language and the culture of His hearers to express spiritual truth. While no one has ever matched the marvelous simplicity of His parables, we can imitate His style. He talked about things that everyone understood; a wayward son, money, lost sheep, laughter and weeping. He "saw' people as they were and lifted them to levels of high expectation by expanding their personal ability to make the better choices.

After the Apostle John wrote twenty-one chapters describing His ministry, there is a choking sensation of inability underlining his attempt to fully communicate it to his readers, "And there are also many other things which Jesus did, the which, if they should be written every one, I suppose that even the world itself could not contain the books that should be written" (John 21:25).

Therefore, it is my consensus that those who seek to minister in Christ's stead, should follow the example He left in the record. Their ministry should be a pattern or a copy of His ministry. The actions of all involved could manifest no greater quality than the characteristics that are synonymous with His work. No activity in which the church should involve itself should be an end to itself, but a means toward the growth of the Body of Christ.

The ministry of the early church was but an extension of what Jesus authorized. They watched Him and duplicated His ministry. In our day we must come to realize that we are but ambassadors of His cause as we reach for the ability to truly minister to our world. In reaching the pinnacles of the achievements of the early church, the fervor and power they demonstrated, is it not reasonable that we should adopt their sacrifices, and mirror their commitment? If we wish to attain the scope of ministry sufficient to evangelize our world, must we not be infused with an insatiable thirst to "become all things to all men" that we might win some? Is there any way we can continue to live a life of affluence, surrounding ourselves with the conveniences of life while ignoring the fact that sacrifice played the greater part of Jesus' ministry? Will we be able to look into His face as he tearfully asks the why's of a finally lost world He had come to save?

The ministry of the early church and the ministry of the United Pentecostal Church is but two parts of the same commission; a commission that will be finished only by the return of our Lord. The mission all have been charged with is that of becoming His witnesses, and carrying the good news of the gospel to the people of all nations. The message is too clear to be mistaken, and the language too explicit to misunderstand. The whole world is our goal... and our responsibility!

In view of this, I am confident that our vision should not be blurred with the ambiguity of our times. As Jesus demonstrated, and the early church duplicated, the gospel penetrated across racial and cultural barriers to reach even the palace in Rome. The beggar on the street, the rich young ruler, the leper's appeal, and the gentile mother in whose arms the ailing child was carried, and the centurion weeping over the pending loss of his daughter. And yes, the Syrophenician was a woman who represented another dispensation, and another culture. Jesus ministered to those who pressed in close to hear. When the evangelized were of another culture, the familiar request, " ...go to your home... to your friends... and tell them what great things the Lord has done for you."

After Pentecost the early church stepped quickly from the upper room to the streets. Newly charged disciples imitated the ministry they had witnessed for three years and a half. The healing of the lame man at the gate called beautiful, Lydia raised to life, the revival in the city of Samaria, the privilege of the gentiles to participate in the church, and the apostle's desire to evangelize Rome.

I would like for you to bear with me as I express my feelings about evangelism. I firmly believe the world has been open to the gospel. I do not feel that our task is an impossible one. It is my opinion, and I admit that openly, that our biggest problem is not without, opposition has always been an instrument of Satan as a deterrent to evangelism. I believe our problem is a self-inflicted injury that brings the negatives into play.

"Go ye therefore into all the world...." Jesus said, as if to respond to the festive attitude that reflects appreciation for a personal salvation experience. This will not be the task of the few, but will be the responsibility of the whole. Clearly all United Pentecostals will need to pull together behind the program if evangelizing the world is to become a reality.

Special responsibility falls to those who neither help nor hinder the evangelism process. Fortunately, there are people who carry the burden meant for all of us.

Although you expect everyone who benefits from the system to rally to the front, it is not a foregone conclusion; everyone simply is not capable to look beyond personal returns and see investments in eternity. Nor can they justify supreme sacrifice on their part to under gird another's opportunity to share in the kingdom. While principle dictates that each cell in the natural body be capable of reproduction, the cells must function for the benefit of the whole body.

The key is for each member to work with precision to extend the church into all the world. We must not maximize failure, nor search for excuse, but obtain and promote a positive vision of the consummated project. Applaud the successes of all men, and participate in their rejoicing. Avoid an investigation to ascertain facts, and promote an attitude "Forbid them not. Those who are not against us are for us."

In evangelism, time must not be wasted casting blame. All issues aside, there is no scapegoat, there is only one problem- us. We must come to the conclusion that to cast blame we self-inflict injury.

Whatever mess exists, we made it. If there are problems, they exist because we have neglected to solve them. Have we been forced to worship in shoddy church buildings while we create lavish lifestyles for ourselves? Have we been dragged into business deals where we become indebted and overextended. Was there someone standing over us with a threat of death to sign consumer notes to thousands of dollars while we struggle to pay tithe and dole out pennies to missions?

There are flaws to be sure, but the real problem is us. We have gotten lazy. Evangelism is hard work. It is sacrificial. It is difficult and ambiguous to those without vision. It requires that we discipline ourselves to competently carry out responsibilities. It requires that we spend quality time fighting impossible odds to plant churches.

Too many of us do not do that. Too many of us do not fully understand the need to plan farther ahead than retirement. Too many of us think that to develop young men for ministry, we are presenting challenges to our popularity or authority.

Evangelism is our responsibility. Our churches are our responsibility. But if we shirk those responsibilities, let us at least take responsibility for our failures and not blame others-least of all those who become the victims of things we do not do.

I can think of no waste as great as that of the ability to evangelize the world, and because we fail to unite our efforts, blame every cause but ourselves. What an awful, undignified waste to bury in the cemetery of what could have been.

When we can get a vision of the world destined for judgment unless we can reach them, the evangelistic activity will actually explode from within! We must become committed....and that today!

Chapter Eighteen
Some Strategy For Multicultural Church Planting

There is a great need in the world for more vibrant evangelistic churches. If we are going to begin thinking seriously about evangelizing the world, we must begin to think about the multiplication of churches.

Did Jesus want to evangelize the world, or did he merely want to start a few churches for the gratification of fellowship tendencies and a profitable business for the professional minister? Was he serious when he mandated the "whole world" as the church's responsibility? Just how did he suppose it to be accomplished? Did he really mean that the ultimate goal of the church was to bring every living person into a personal relationship with God?

The fact is that for too long these questions have been conveniently placed into mental files reserved for serious consideration....but at a later date. As a church, we must address world evangelism now! It is already late.

There is no mystery surrounding the fact that world evangelism begins at the local level. To expand around the world, we must first grow domestically. We must plant churches with the expectation that they grow- and fast. We must multiply our existing congregations, and motivate every capable believer to think in terms of ministry. For too long we have thought in terms of pulpit mastery when we thought of ministry, but ministry is also a layman's word. It is a commission to serve. It is the responsibility of every believer to get involved in church planting- the need to plant churches has reached a level of crisis.

Never has there been a clear mission strategy more needed than today. Something that will fall in line with apostolic methods. The fervor of the apostolic fathers to expand the perimeters of the church became themes of municipal debate as their results stirred cities to the roots; they turned their world upside down. Modern church philosophy has leaned more to maintaining what it has accomplished, leaving little thought to increase. We have been so occupied by domestic house keeping, that very few gates of hell have been rattled. Evangelizing even the back-doors of our churches is too awesome, too ugly, too costly. In too many cases the church has been lured by the temptation to invest efforts in other than evangelism.

The church can build a wall, board up the windows, plan just to survive, or it can move aggressively into the streets to present the gospel of Jesus Christ to people- all kinds of people. Coming from behind the luxury of stained glass is the only obvious route to meet the needs of the lost, and produce automatic results to impact our world.

There are men in shops, sales positions, office complexes, behind the wheel of a big rig, working as medical doctors or lawyers, and a myriad of other professions that need to be impacted with the need to start churches. Gideon was harvesting crops... James and John were fishing.... Matthew was collecting taxes.... And, who was the polite gentleman merely sitting under the fig tree?

The world's greatest evangelist was a converted lawyer. He traveled in company of a medical doctor. Of the 12 apostles, eleven were Galileans- country people who spoke with an accent. The social order scorned some of the church's leaders as ignorant and unlearned, but the Book of Acts tells us that these men united their efforts and started churches. The teachings of Christ spread rapidly by a united thrust of evangelism. The common people heard them gladly, but also "of the chief priests and scribes not a few."

When we speak of church planting, we must talk about natural church growth, which means, church planting from the local inter-city structure. Churches can spread through a city and across a land if the will is present to allow it to happen. Society determines or strongly influences every aspect of what a man says, thinks, and does. Consequently, the change will have to come from the social order of the church on location. When we learn the local church's attitude on evangelism, we will know how church planting is likely to increase and spread through it's community. If everyone would effectively evangelize his own back door, the world evangelism question would have its solution.

For the United Pentecostal Church International this is no time for fun and games. At some point we are going to have to put world evangelism on the priority list where it can influence us, motivate us, and nip at our heels until we reach our world.

I was in Central America recently for the purpose of teaching a pastoral development seminar. As I stood among ministers who had committed themselves to the task of the ministry, many of them suffering extreme abuse, I felt so fortunate to share precious moments with them. What a privilege, what an honor, what an inspiration I felt as I ministered under the inspiration of the holy anointing of God!

Pouring my heart into those services I thought, "How much vitality is here! How much triumph! How much love! Simple biblical truths brought tears of gratitude to their eyes. They strained to catch every word falling from my lips. No preacher ever had a more deserving or more appreciative congregation. Their desire for the word of God made the task of ministering to them both sacramental and joyous.

When these men had a rest break, they prayed! I listened to their simple appeals with a hush permeating my mind. They prayed that God would plant the material they had learned into their lives to empower them to the work. One goal could be easily detected, "Churches,""they moaned, "We need more churches that we might reach more people! Give us men to augment our ability to start more churches!" To hear them pray was to experience the very presence of God. They had translated my teaching to a level of action; an action that began to drive them. I realized with that kind of impact it would only be a short while until the spoken lessons would be put into service. I was both cast down with the knowledge that I had not prayed with that kind of conviction for quite some time, and lifted up that God had inspired me in spite of it, to teach that which could be translated to burden.

I envisioned a comparison of these men and women and those of the homeland. Having been a missionary, I knew their sacrifices. Many of them pastored churches while living under threats of death. Cruel beatings inflicted by their peers was evident by physical scars. Only God knew and understood the emotional scars that were also present in their hearts. Yet what they are doing cannot be destroyed! Not by all the forces of evil that rage against them. That evil has attacked for no other reason than that these pastors represent the church- the church the homeland takes so many times for granted. Planting churches for them is a mandate, it is also a privilege, and they will do it in spite of all opposition.

These men, and others like them who form the outreach of the United Pentecostal Church around the world, demonstrate that the message will penetrate any given barrier, even if doors are closed, pastors are thrown in jail, persecution is intense, and devils rampant.

I left the seminar praying more earnestly for something to get down on the inside of us on the home front; something that will match their sacrifice and equal their burden. The great commission does not present an option, rather an ultimatum. And planting churches any where in the world fulfills that ultimatum.

To plant churches we must infuse method. Paul's approach to plant church was often centered on particular families. From reading the accounts of his ministry, it appears that he would find the key member of a family through which he could communicate his messages to the other members of that family. In his writings he greeted the household of various believers, wherein was contained more often than not, a congregation, a church. Further study indicates that Paul utilized this same method of communication to his advantage as he established doctrine and maintained the members of the churches he had planted.

For those involved in church planting, the dynamics of the family enhances the success pattern. Workers among most multicultural believers will invariably find it necessary to deal with the family. Among these cultures, even though family members may be separated by great distances, the family circle continues to carry a great deal of influence. Contact may be interrupted at times, but it is not broken. Family influence is brought into play when decisions are being made, for any decision in these cultures affects the total family. When one member of a family is converted, the church usually will incorporate the total family, or else find it difficult to retain the new member.

Is this method of extending the message through the family and friendship network Bible based? Yes, most certainly! It was one of the principal tools used by successful early church leaders. When a member of a household was baptized, through the new believer entire families were brought into the fellowship.

Cornelius was evangelized by Simon Peter. When the Holy Ghost fell on those whom Cornelius had gathered to hear the message, the Scripture informs us that the entire household was baptized. When the jailer of Philippi asked Paul and Silas what he needed to do to be saved, he was told to believe upon the Lord Jesus Christ with his house. When the word of the Lord was explained, the jailer was baptized, he and his house. A woman called Lydia, a seller of purple, believed with her household. Her house became the meeting place for the church in that city.

Jason and his house at Thessalonica was a focal point for the church in that city. There was Justus of Corinth, a Gentile, who had a house adjacent to the synagogue. The church that met in his house was possibly the means by which Crispus, the chief ruler of the synagogue, believed on the Lord with all his house. Further results were gleaned by this household, for many of the Corinthians heard the word from that house, believed, and were baptized. It is a principle that by being utilized to the maximum, develops a pattern for spiritual reproduction.

In the epistles Paul wrote, he had certain communications for households. It is probable that these households were won to the Lord through a key member who had been reached and won to the faith. The influence of that member resulted in other family members being baptized, and each person in his own right provided keys to additional families and friends. Thus the church in apostolic days multiplied.

It is evident that Paul's strategy was guided by the Holy Ghost. The churches he planted grew and multiplied. His converts became extensions of his ministry, and developed into mature men and women who would give up their lives but not their faith. Witnessing was spontaneous. No one had to send them out; they merely went into the street to make history for the cause.

These accounts teach us that church planting was married to household evangelism. Where we find references to a family having been reached, we generally find that a church was planted in that house. Buildings were superfluous to the congregations of early church days. The major emphasis was placed upon the growth of a congregation and reaching a city for Christ.

Church planting dominated the thinking of productive evangelists in those days. They willingly made personal sacrifices in order to obtain their goals, and their love for the kingdom of God was evident by those sacrifices. Position and fame did not interest them in the least. They placed no importance upon the person, only on the purpose. Spiritual results were the desire and heartbeat of the believer. Of course, there emerged leaders as the administration and care of the congregation began to call for such, but extending the kingdom was the thought that permeated their minds. Control of the ever extending church was not a priority; that was relegated to a secondary responsibility.

Who would administrate what was lost in the exhaust fumes of evangelism? The early church somehow never got around to separating the activities of soulwinning from church administration and church planting. The power-packed messengers of the gospel attracted hungry hearts, and new converts were charged with the fires of evangelism. It seems that every member became an evangelist, duplicating their experiences in the lives of others. Evangelism was the fire that warmed the soul, and early church fathers whipped it into flaming infernos that raced through their world, pouring the gospel into the household. Each house, saturated with the Holy Ghost, became a milestone as the church pushed back the frontiers. Each household became a living cell of fellowship, worship, and service.

Our strategy, especially in the Latin culture, is focusing upon this principle. We are sharply accenting family responsibility. A greater hunger to extend the kingdom is coming to the surface. As new souls are reached, a consuming force is planted within, sending them as a witness to family and friends. Again, more often than not, a congregation emerges out of the generated enthusiasm.

There is a negative to this method, expressed with some credibility by leaders who fear for new believers who are brought to spiritual birth without leadership. However, if we again use the New Testament method as our example, we will find that it was this principle that created the need for the epistles to be written. Paul was the professed and confessed pastor. The master of the house was often the spiritual leader and recipient of Paul's letters of instruction to the church that, more often than not, met in his house.

Church planting began with the family. When new souls outside the household were reached, it appears that they met with the members of that house. They, in turn, provided new contact points for the advancement of the gospel. They became living links to a human network of families in an ever-lengthening chain. The result was a people conductor that allowed the currents of the gospel to flow to distant points, providing energy for evangelism.

Were there problems? Of course there were problems. Some of them were serious, and are exposed in Paul's letters. But, they did not slow down the church-planting process any more than problems among children in a human family stop childbearing. The family network was maintained, well lubricated, and utilized. Today's church leaders, hungry for results, could learn much by reading the New Testament from this perspective.

Is there a clear reason why we should adopt this method of evangelism in spite of the risks involved? I believe there is. While it is only one of the many tools available to the church today, I believe it is the most effective ever utilized. It is a natural conveyance for the gospel. It is very much like the network of copper wiring used to supply electricity for the home. Wherever the wires come in contact with a ground, the current will flow, breaking out in as many areas as the network is extended. Likewise, the pulpit sends out the charges, and the family network carries the current to perform the purpose; many times an incredible distance from the source of the message. As invisible wires carry the electricity behind the scenes, so a network of family and friends plugs into the activity and sends it to whatever area the family happens to have contact.

We must, while using this method, be aware that there is a distinct responsibility of administration. When evangelistic contacts cross areas of administration, ethical guidelines must be followed. There are rules of conduct that govern activity for the purpose of harmony and productivity.

While we must not violate the ethics of administration while performing evangelism, neither should administration hinder the extending of the kingdom by evangelism. Administration can fail to apprehend opportunities for growth if it persists in maintaining wrong attitudes toward evangelism. There are times when well-meaning policies clash when dealing with methods and results. Yet when the great commission to the church is the priority, administration and evangelism can eradicate any pending problem and bring about smooth operation. This is not only possible, but necessary to the work of God worldwide. When people are allowed to evangelize- when this becomes the priority- the faith can spread, bringing healthy growth to our churches.

Rules and laws of operation in the body become policy or principles of conduct. No well-meaning person in the body would intentionally violate any of these rules, for to do so undermine harmony. However, when doing the work of evangelism, the end result and motive must be considered. People with the church's best interest at heart- an interest that outweighs personal involvement- will understand those motives, and move to harmonize the extended limits with administration policy.

The family network, since it is not knowledgeable of church structure, at times will cross administrational boundaries. Sensitive leaders will seek within ethical guidelines, first to evangelize the household, and afterward to incorporate it into the church body. The continued process will include administration, which will guide it into spiritual maturity.

We are the same church, whether we deal in evangelism or in administration. We are laboring together for the same desired goals. If soulwinning and church planting to extend God's kingdom is sincerely the motive of all involved, neither evangelism nor administration will be made prisoner of the other. All will be happy for the advancement of the church body and will work together to blend efforts into continuity. It simply will not matter from what source the results are produced. We must not ignore the harvest in the field because we cannot agree on the methods used in the storehouse, lest the harvest be lost. If, on the other hand, motives are not correct, a problem exists apart from soulwinning activity.

Some methods can stifle, or hinder the great possibilities for evangelism. That is why it would be very hard to improve upon New Testament methods of propagation. I am very happy with our organization's administrative efforts, for administration must be utilized to mold personnel into a smoothly operating organism. We must be guided by the Holy Ghost to yield to what is being produced by our hard working constituency.

On the other hand, Spirit filled men and women must continue to produce growing, productive churches, and if methods begin to be counterproductive for the overall purpose of the church and do not serve us well, those methods need to be dispensed with and more effective methods adopted. We must be fair in our assessment of present methods and weigh our results. If an program of evangelism is producing, it must continue to receive our support. But, there is no place among us for a faltering activity that does not generate souls for the kingdom. Our world missions purpose cannot be defined by any other terms. Our purpose is to evangelize the world, and that must have priority over any feeling of loyalty to unproductive programs-no matter to whom they belong. We are racing time to the rapture while world population is outstripping us.

Chapter Nineteen
The Plan

The United Pentecostal Church is commissioned to reach its total community with the gospel of Jesus Christ. And, as the past records will support, the church has had a very effective outreach. However, changes have dictated that evangelism methods be updated to balance the changes the community has undergone over the past fifteen years. The once totally Anglo neighborhood is now home to Hispanics, Laotians, Hmongs, and Middle Easterners. It is a foregone truth that the church must have an adjustment of attitude in order to create successful evangelism programs that will impact the new community.

The United Pentecostal Church quite some time ago initiated innovative interaction about cross-cultural outreach. Demographic studies revealed many of our cities were populated by a majority of ethnic language cultures; a fact that produced serious consideration to modify strategy. In as much as all people are sensitive to culture and language, it was decided that language and culture would be an effective tool of evangelism. Also, it became more and more evident that the multicultural community wished to worship and study the Bible in the language that best communicated with their understanding (A person's first or primary language). Therefore, it became obvious that strategy should be adjusted to utilize distinctive languages in the evangelism process. The bottom line resulted in cross-culture evangelism.

Once evangelized, our ethnic cultures fill our churches with faithful saints. Out of the results men will be called to minister, and that most generally to like kind. Many will return to homelands out of a burning desire to carry the message to family and friends; many of those living in obscure areas of the world Christ commissioned the church to evangelize. From whatever angle one chooses to evaluate cross-culture evangelism, it is a positive step to reach our world.

One method of cross-cultural outreach is to share facilities with an multicultural congregation; another is to give birth to one. Unfortunately sharing is inherently difficult for humans, and change not one of our most admirable traits. To involve the congregation in sharing the facility, and changing attitude to successfully follow-through, perhaps a few facts and suggestions will be appreciated.

North America has more unchurched people than all other countries except Russia, China, and India. The reason is that of immigration. Therefore the growing ethnicity of the United States requires that many of the new congregations must be a multicultural one; a fact especially true in California, New York, Florida, and the provinces of Quebec, Ontario, New

Brunswick, and British Columbia, Canada.

More than 500 ethnic groups among 100 million United States residents now identify themselves as people who speak another language. I feel sure this fact would extend to Canada as well. This growing ethnicity creates an urgency to begin and assist emerging multicultural congregations.

The birth and growth of any new congregation is initially a struggle for survival. Membership is small, finances limited, and leaders scarce. Increasing land prices and zoning restrictions also limit the availability of property and buildings for multicultural congregations. Some Anglo congregations have buildings with space that could be used for an multicultural daughter congregation, or an emerging multicultural congregation on the short-term. These congregations could use the space on Sunday afternoons, or any given night of the week. Sharing buildings makes good business sense, and even better strategy for evangelism. It also proves that we are better stewards of buildings dedicated to Christ. A daughter congregation will rise to call a mother church blessed.

Many times only a suggestion is necessary to open a wide world of possibility to a struggling church as it endeavors to evangelize the total community. The changing face of demographics tells us that many of our communities reflect a larger percentage of cultural language groups than that of the usual white-English. When some churches were begun some time ago, the emphasis was different. However, the purpose of the church has never changed! God planted the church in that community to evangelize it- not just like kind, but every creature.

The need to understand God's ways is great! The church must educate its congregation that secular feelings are not sufficient to withhold evangelism.

Some feel the ethnic group understands English, and has little need for special language supplement. Others openly express that they are in North America now and should speak English. A no and a yes should answer those questions. Religion has a specialized vocabulary. Some ethnics with a good grasp of general English vocabulary have problems understanding "church language". Due to immigration from a myriad of cultures around the world, much of the local community the church is reaching today is not from a Christian background, and may apply different definitions to a Christian vocabulary. Therefore language and custom are very effective in eliminating these ambiguities.

As far as they are living in a dominant English society, every immigrant will evolve in time, and if not the first generation immigrant, then certainly the generations who follow. It's difficult to phrase a proper answer, but, if we spend millions to evangelize in foreign countries, should we neglect them as neighbors?

There is yet another, and more significant factor. As the first generation Spanish (or any minority language group) begins to function in the dominant English environment of North America, they understand little or no English. We have a responsibility to reach them with the gospel. Therefore, we present the gospel in the language of the targeted culture. Our churches initiate a second congregation using that language to evangelize, disciple, and train the converts. As the children study in English schools, play with English speaking friends, and become involved with the local youth group of the English ccongregation, they will become more comfortable in an English environment. The benefits of a one church concept comes into focus. The children will become a part of the English activities, and not fall through the proverbial cracks. The church has won members by automatic association, and without additional evangelism.

People prefer to come to Jesus by crossing the fewest number of linguistic, social, and racial barriers. For this reason the church will rise to meet the challenge and make whatever changes are necessary to "become all things to all men' and win some.

When questions of concern have been raised by sincere pastors, there is an answer for them. Let us see if we can pose the hypothetical question to your advantage.

"I want to evangelize my community of ethnic cultures but I do not feel I can pastor them. What can I do?"

Moving this option quickly out of the way will eliminate the need to elaborate in depth over activity that the pastor will not be involved in. The answer is very simple. The local church remains responsible to the total community, and certain principles are in effect. The church must be a fountain of life for the community, or it is failing in its purpose. Therefore, a presentation of the gospel for the variegated community must be provided. This is the only valid reason for the church's existence. Therefore, my advice would be: That after a time of prayer devoted to the burden for the community, the pastor should create a task force to study the demographics of the neighborhood. If the present congregation is not large, the pastor may wish to do this study personally. These answers are available in the county library in the reference department. Just tell the librarian that you wish to learn the demographics of the city. After ascertaining the demographic makeup, prayer can then can be directed more effectively to the burden.

If the area in which the church is located has a considerable second culture, that should be the ethnic culture that the church should focus upon.

The pastor, before sharing his burden with the church family, should ask God to direct him to a struggling pastor of that culture, or who has linguistic abilities to adequately reach the people of that language, and consider opening the church's facility to an multicultural sister family. A time of conversation will determine if the answers are all available before actually implementing action.

This option demands that the sister church is registered by the state. Articles of incorporation must be drawn up and presented to the Secretary of State. A tax number must be applied for, and extended by the Internal Revenue Service, and an adequate bookkeeping method adopted by the emerging congregation. The pastor of the mother church will give advice in these matters, but will not be responsible for the finances nor the shepherding of the second flock.

If the pastor of the second congregation is of the quality that can adequately carry this responsibility, a simple explanation will begin putting together a workable plan where the mother church continues to evangelize the dominant culture while the second congregation will evangelize the minority culture from the same facility. In this manner the church is fulfilling its purpose.

The pastor may wish to extend to the sister congregation a "free rent' policy for a year, or until the congregation matures sufficiently to assist in the financial burden of a church facility. A written plan called an agreement should be drawn up. The presbyter should be involved, or the director of Multicultural Ministries. The church should have autonomous status in the section, and listed in the manual. The plan should spell out the desires of the mother church as it pertains to cleaning, maintenance, participation, and what financial obligations are involved. Remember we are talking about evangelizing the total community-your community!.

"I want to establish a daughter congregation and in time plant it as a daughter church in the community"

This option is the more popular, since it deals with a more intimate approach and a continued relationship. Very few problems have evolved from establishing a daughter congregation in the same facility the mother church occupies when certain guidelines have been followed. The procedure is relatively simple, but one that demands that the pastor and the congregation adopt a new mentality. The daughter congregation must not be considered a burden, rather a fountain of life for another culture. The new converts will be a part of the church, not apart from the church. They will merely be the part of the congregation that speaks another language, and as such, demands special attention. They are an indispensable action of the church to reach the total community of the city.

After a time of prayer the pastor should begin searching for a spiritual son that has the capabilities to reach the minority group abounding in the "back yard' of the church. When the personnel has been properly selected, without revealing purpose, the pastor should begin "pouring' himself into the aspiring person. He should become a mentor to this person until there is a relationship developed that will sustain the future plan.

When the time is right, and after a time of prayer together, the pastor should reveal his plan. I must reach this community, he should explain, and this is the way I wish to do it. Then the pastor should explain the design that has been mentally developed. From the beginning the future multicultural church should be considered a daughter congregation, and whatever it takes to nurture it and bring it to maturity, should be considered a part of the program. As in the previous option, an agreement should be drawn up and signed. It will serve as a reminder of the dynamics of the plan, and provide securities against misunderstanding.

The status of the personnel should be considered. A future position on the ministerial staff is the more successful option in this regard. In this manner the planning for the daughter congregation is always under the supervision of the administration. Furthermore, the cost of operations is made a common factor, and there will be proper communication of this to the daughter congregation, who should have an opportunity to share in the expense load.

Finances should be run through the financial records of the mother church as in the manner of any department of the church. Offerings should be considered common revenue for the operation of the facility. If the church does not need the added revenue, it should consider a savings account set aside for the day when the daughter is "married", and planted in the community. Tithing proceeding from the new converts of the daughter congregation should be kept in a separate account, and a plan initiated for providing a subsidy to the emerging "pastor" of the group. Some senior pastors accommodate the junior pastor with all the tithes of newly gained converts, or a percentage of them, while the tithes of any pre-existing members continue to be recorded in the regular tithing account. Special occasions when additional offerings are needed, the daughter congregation should be given the opportunity to assist according to their abilities.

The junior pastor should be given the responsibility to be an under shepherd. Visitation of the sick, evangelism follow-up, visitor follow-up, and regular pastoral responsibility teach the emerging minister to be responsible. Domestic counseling, membership encouragement, etc., should be accomplished under the tutoring of the senior pastor, and recognized as accountable duties of the junior pastor. A full report of activity should be required until such time the congregation is planted.

The junior pastor's wife should be taken into account. When ladies' functions are planned, the culture should be taken into consideration. If the function is for all the ladies, the daughter church should be automatically included, remembering that certain customs may not be as interesting to them. However, given time, they can learn. If customs differ in certain activities, such as baby showers and birthday gatherings, it might be advisable to invite the ladies of the sister congregation to these functions, while granting opportunity for the event to be programmed in the culture of the congregation affected. At any rate, the senior pastor's wife would be wise to always include the junior pastor's wife, not only as a matter of training, but also of incorporating cultural flavor into the church family.

Schedules are important for both congregations. A calendar of events should be maintained. This is covered in the next chapter.

The developing minister should be mentored into the licensing process. Local license should be sought, and assistance given to see that the ministerial application is properly filled out and submitted to the presbyter. Granting a local license does not diminish the pastor's responsibility, nor does it take the emerging minister away from the senior pastor's authority. The aspiring minister should have the right to be involved in the licensing process. At the time for planting the church, the senior pastor shall make sure that proper procedure has been followed to have the church recognized in the district, and before property is purchased, rented, or donated, approvals have been secured from the District Board for the location of the daughter congregation. A big celebration of the event will insure a proper relationship for the future. As a daughter being married, the congregation will always be a daughter, but the responsibilities will take on a different approach. After "planting" the daughter church, plans should be under way for the mother church to begin yet another daughter congregation. In this manner the church fulfills its obligations for existence.

The time for planting the daughter church should be mutually agreed upon. Not with a time schedule, rather with an achievement accomplishment. Growth should be taken into account, and financial ability of the congregation indispensable. Mutual bonds of fellowship should continue between the two congregations.

"I want to evangelize the ethnic cultures of my community utilizing my present facilities, but I need cultural expertise."

The same path that leads to the former option should be followed by the pastor who desires to always contain the daughter congregation in the mother church facility. A modification can be made in the agreement that will provide for the future, such as financial arrangements for the junior pastor, and the clear understanding that the second congregation will remain a part of the mother church. The junior pastor can in time become a "fulltime" assistant by building into the program an adequate financial plan. This arrangement never hurts a senior pastor because most likely the rapidly growing cultural membership would not otherwise exist. However, the advantage of a financial plan is that it provides incentives for dedication. The pastor who desires that the daughter congregation always occupy the facility of the mother church is using this method to evangelizing his total community. He can house as many cultural congregations as the church has facility to contain them. A note of warning would be that care is given to have adequate space and schedule to properly develop any additional cultural daughter congregation. Also special attention should be given that the privileges are not merely to accommodate another congregation, it is the purpose of evangelism that is being served. It is to the church's credit that the community is being evangelized. The responsibility is already upon the shoulders of the mother church.

Chapter Twenty
Sharing Facilities With A Daughter Church

The sharing of facilities can be one of the greatest opportunities in which a church can serve its community. It can realize the success of reaching the total community, and at the same time bring added flavor into the mother church by incorporating cultural values that will enhance the beauty of diversity.

However, pitfalls are many. There will be problems, but if the mother church will develop an attitude concerning the daughter congregation as that of a mother giving birth, and developing a natural daughter to maturity, the responsibility will become a challenge rather than a hazard.

Problems usually have solutions for the individual, or the church, that desires to solve the problem. When a mentality to rid one's self of responsibility exists, there is no real desire for a solution. Notwithstanding the challenge, a beautiful relationship with a daughter congregation of a minority language will give the world a demonstration of God's love. He came to reach a world, and He gave himself to the task. People will remember the service the mother congregation has rendered to its cultural responsibility. The world knows it is not easy, but by successfully working side by side, it proves the church is a body in which there is no respect of persons.

Let me suggest an agenda for considering a second congregation sharing the local facility:

Purpose: Dedicated church buildings are used as a sanctuary in which to worship God. These buildings must be used to a maximum, and many times this means reaching out to a community of a different language. Sometimes we must choose between evangelism and entertainment, or between evangelism and secondary services the church may render its community. Souls must be seen as the priority, and this means the most productive outreach method must be utilized.

Meeting Place: The second congregation will need adequate space in order to be successful. If parking poses a problem, consider an alternating schedule that will not conflict. While advantageous to meet during the mother church's Sunday service schedule, if a sufficient area is not available, a multicultural congregation would be delighted to meet on Sunday afternoon. Appropriate signs to announce the second language congregation are necessary, and it is important that care be shown in their design in order to demonstrate pride in the presence of a second congregation.

Relationship: When two distinct groups share, sometimes the second congregation becomes a scapegoat for every imaginary problem. It is easy to think "they' were responsible, or even if the case is obvious, relationship must be created to a point that both are laborers together for the same cause. The church is evangelizing the total community, and any multicultural congregation is a vital part of the overall plan. Friendship will minimize stress points, and in most cases, eliminate it.

Maintenance: Many times a second congregation is asked only to handle cleaning limited to their particular function. Eventually, a sharing of a salaried custodian is perhaps the better method. Cleaning supplies, paper products, and utensils should be considered, and responsibilities clearly stated.

Government: If a second congregation is a daughter of the mother church, thorough examination should be given to government. Most generally an assistant benefiting percentage-wise financially from growth pattern will produce both in loyalty and number for the emerging daughter church. Relationship to the mother congregation must be determined early, and not left to result in misunderstanding. An ownership attitude is not a very productive relationship, rather working together to affect the total community.

If the second congregation is merely sharing the space, agreements should be written out and fully understood by mediation before the function begins. Each consideration should favor the possibility of evangelism, and not financial gain. The purpose is not to merely benefit the mother congregation financially, but to adequately evangelize the community. A small emerging congregation will succeed if given understanding and love.

Responsibilities: Everything that is expected of the second congregation should be discussed openly, and put in writing. Written agreements must be understood as an avenue for understanding, and not as a tool for enforcement. The attitude that is woven into the agreement produces a will to conform to principles involved.

Conflict: Where there are people, there will be problems! But like any family, one must learn to resolve conflict in mutually satisfactory terms. Preemptive planning will streamline conflict-resolution process between the two congregations. This process should include periodic preset times for both congregations to evaluate the relationship and the written agreements. An insurance for harmony would be the appointment of a person from each congregation to be designated to receive and act upon complaints. When a problem arises, the designated person will discuss the problem with the appropriate counterpart.

Finances and budget control: If the second congregation is a daughter congregation, the host congregation does not calculate giving birth to a church as a mere investment: It is an outreach to the total community. A productive arrangement is for the pastor of the daughter congregation to be a member of the pastoral staff, therefore knowledgeable of cost control. The daughter congregation's finances merely flows into the financial structure of the mother church. It is always productive to provide financial benefit from positive outreach for the second congregation.

If the program calls for the multicultural congregation to be planted in the community, and another daughter congregation initiated, some churches find it helpful to provide the facilities free for the first year- then set aside a predetermined percentage of the funds of the daughter congregation for a down-payment on real property so they can begin moving toward self-support and self-government.

If the second congregation is merely sharing the building, the host congregation may wish to follow the same guidelines the first year, and then charge the second congregation a predetermined monthly rental that rises according to the financial stability of the second. More than one church has subsidized its operating budget with proceeds from a second congregation. However, the emphasis must be kept upon purpose:evangelism!

Activity Calendar: A church calendar of events should be displayed in a predetermined place. The events that are approved and scheduled by respective planning committees are followed through according to the calendar. This system breaks down if either congregation disregards the calendar as an unimportant responsibility.

Worship styles: Ethnics worship Jesus in ways that reflect their culture. This includes their music, length of service, and order of service. The multicultural congregation should be given autonomy to worship freely without pressure to conform to another cultural preference. That worship style will include their individual ways of observing ordinances such as the Lord's supper, etc.

Termination of the relationship: At some point the multicultural congregation may outgrow the facility, or mutually agree that productive evangelism could be enhanced by separation from the mother congregation. The spiritual bond should never be broken, or congregations should not allow adverse feelings to develop that necessitates the second congregation to feel isolated, or the mother congregation be taken advantage of. A mutually agreed-upon procedure is therefore essential. Allow the daughter congregation/guest congregation sufficient time to find a new place to meet.

On rare occasions congregations become incompatible. That generally occurs when written agreements are nonexistent or disregarded. Again proper follow-through procedure should be built in for protection, and never be acted upon out of disrespect, no matter the problem. It is Christ's church, and his purpose for which we operate.

In some areas of our fellowship, a mother church has given birth to as many as four daughter congregations using the same facilities. Others have observed the option of planting the congregation as a daughter congregation in the community and initiating another daughter congregation using the same spiritual "womb".

The benefits to a mother congregation and the emerging congregation far outweigh the disadvantages. The challenges and the inconveniences are rewarded, as many ethnics in the community accept Jesus Christ as Savior. Love replaces years of prejudice and friendship replaces stereotype. Both the mother congregation and the multicultural congregations are blessed for their participation in the Great Commission.

Then There Is The Bi-lingual Church

Many of our English-speaking churches are sitting on top of a wealth of souls. There are as many as 48 million Spanish people living in North America, and only five percent of them reported as evangelical Christians. They represent a ripe harvest field. Many English speaking congregations have a strong desire to evangelize Hispanics but simply do not know how. Yet nowhere can the love of Christ be more evident- the oneness of his purpose more visible, and the gospel more dramatic-than in the mixing of the world's cultures into one body. Therefore, let us use Spanish as an example second congregation. The result will be His church whatever the second culture!

It is possible for English and Spanish speakers to worship in the same church, and according to the degree of assimilation, even in the same service. English-speaking soul winners are learning that with a little tolerance of language and culture, even those not yet assimilated can be won by our efforts. However, we must be prewarned that Satan will attempt to use this wonderful activity to further divide the church. Using racial bias or cultural differences in his deceitful scheming, he can hinder a world-wide revival in the making.

A word of caution should be given to the church that is interested in establishing a bi-lingual congregation: It is better not to enter into cross-culture evangelism than to do so in a halfhearted manner. A pastor's good intentions running aground can greatly harm the original purpose.

A pastor must first convince his congregation of his program and solicit his people's help. After initiating the work he must be prepared to take time to develop a leader. It is a work of patience and perseverance, but one that pays great dividends.

If the church is considering a bi-lingual approach, instead of merely sharing the facilities of a local congregation, we are considering a total assimilation. This option is also open to pastors and churches that desire to become involved in cross-culture evangelism. This deals with implementing an organizational plan.

First, the interested pastor should envision the completed task, and develop an organizational structure best suited to his administrative style. Then he must take a step by faith. He must realize that he will never totally Americanize another culture. Freedom for cultural changes are necessary to the spiritual growth of a bilingual church. The pastor should ask himself, "Will I be comfortable with a bilingual approach in this outreach, or will I demand that all our converts learn English?"

Should the pastor try to learn the language of his intended bi-lingual congregation? In most cases probably not, at least not fluently, for his time will be too limited and the process too long. But there are already many spiritual sons waiting to be born who can become his extended ministry to their culture. This is what the gospel is all about!

A number of other questions need to be addressed. The options addressed in the previous potion of this book should be studied, and a prayerful choice of direction be made. Whether the local church establishes a bi-lingual congregation that will always remain a part of the mother church, or establishes a daughter congregation that becomes autonomous after it reaches maturity, the church should never close the door to future options. With God's help, each option can be equally successful. Where the necessary ingredient of cultural understanding is constantly manifested and Christian love is displayed, any church can become bi-lingual. The church should not close any door that will result in souls won to the body of Christ.

The suggestions gleaned from the experiences of brethren who are launching cross-cultural efforts are invaluable. Of course, any local pastor may develop a better option as he experiments in cross-cultural evangelism.

The first and obvious choice is to have two services in the same church as is indicated by the suggestions in this book, one in English and the other in the minority language. These services meet the individual needs of each group while developing a togetherness that helps to assimilate families. The first generation immigrants prefer to hear the Word of God spoken in his heart language, or the language of his birth. They also feel more comfortable in their own particular style of worship.

The daughter congregation option provides for English-speaking children of unilingual minority parents who attend the church to become incorporated into the main flow by automatic association. The church will glean additional contacts through the family network, and many other potential converts that are available from these families. A wealth of resource becomes immediately available.

Where there is a one-church two-service approach, the pastor is the authority for both cultural groups. If there is a church board, the church should consider including representatives from the minority constituency. All the members will enjoy equal membership rights, regardless of their language preference. If the pastor is bilingual he can communicate with both, otherwise he can communicate through a mediator.

An additional ministry of the church membership could be to provide language training for those minorities who lack the ability to speak the dominant language. This work will involve some people in the church who may not otherwise have a ministry. The pastor should teach the minorities that in order to compete in the adopted culture, it is advisable to learn the language. A person must be able to communicate if he wishes to excel. Offering linguistic classes is also an opportunity to invite the unsaved, who may then be evangelized.

One Church - One Congregation

For the pastor considering the bilingual approach, the total constituency meet in the same service, regardless of culture or language. The services are translated into the languages of the people who are present. Usually, worship and preliminaries are conducted in the predominate culture's language but worship choruses are taught the general congregation who join in the worship of a second language. The sermon is then translated either directly from the pulpit or by mechanical devices. Simultaneous translation by a bilingual person who stands by the speaker should be animated and delivered in the same style as the speaker. Although this activity presents an inexperienced person some apprehension, it is not nearly as difficult as it seems.

Mechanical equipment ranges from a simple amplifier and earphones, to a radio-frequency transmitter. In each case, the translator can have a private set of earphones connected directly into the sound system. This enables him to monitor the pulpit without background noise. He then speaks the translated material into a microphone connected either to the amplifier or the transmitter. The amplifier-earphone method demands that the recipients sit in a close proximity to facilitate the earphone connections. In the transmitter method, they may sit where they choose, tuning their personal radio receiver to the frequency of the miniature broadcast. The best hearing device for the recipient is a double earplug or miniature earphones.

The benefits of this style of service is that all meet together at the same time and participate together as a spiritual family. It requires a bilingual pastor or an assistant who will work faithfully by his side. The one negative is that services can become longer than usual if they are interpreted from the pulpit, due to content repetition. While this is acceptable to the multicultural congregation, it might be taxing to the average English congregation. An evaluation of the long-range effects is advisable.

Since the bottom line objective is to extend the kingdom of God, every local assembly should at least consider the possibility of sharing facilities with a second, minority language congregation. However, many pastors do not wish to involve themselves in cross-culture evangelism due to the unexpected. If so, it would be admirable to confess this and seek another way to serve the kingdom relative to another culture.

Many of our minority language pastors are not financially able to move into a city, rent a building, and pay the expenses of light, water, and heat while supporting a family. Frustration has turned many powerful ethnic ministers away for the lack of a facility. Since every church usually has some days of the week when the windows are dark, or when it conducts some program of minor importance that could be moved to another time or location, the congregation should consider allowing an multicultural congregation to be born in the English church womb.

Even assimilating minorities into one English service is not impossible. For example, minority language people need to practice their English and will thus be forced to learn more rapidly. However, more love and understanding is required to insure those of another culture that the congregation really desires that they be a part, and more assistance is necessary so that they can understand. Most immigrant people living in the U.S. are progressing to some degree in becoming efficient in English. At the same time, the church must accept- without adverse feeling- the decision of many ethnic families who would find this arrangement unacceptable.

Making minority language people comfortable in the local church setting is not difficult. A pastor will attract more than he would have dreamed merely by demonstrating a genuine love toward those of another culture. Here are some additional ideas for the English-speaking pastor.

Give the ethnic believers of the church high visibility. For example, have them participate. The talented can be asked to sing or play musical instruments. Using another language for solos is an interesting idea. Many English-speaking people enjoy another's style of singing.

Invite qualified minority language preachers in whom you have confidence to share the pulpit with you. This should be done without calling attention to the fact; merely allow for a free flow of God's presence. A unique approach is to have reverse translation for English-speaking people. Many of our United Pentecostal Church pastors do this with amazing success.

Devise programs and ideas to use ethnic individuals without appearing condescending to their population. Make it sincere as if it is first nature, and soon it will become so.

Putting the Dream Into Practice

Probably the first major step the English pastor must take after prayer, is to select the proper leadership for the program. The success of the work depends as much on the person or persons leading the outreach as it does the pastor who desires to make it happen. Let me repeat, the pastor should pour himself into an ethnic convert of his own making- one he has prayed for and whom God has given him. This convert will not just develop automatically; the pastor must go out with purpose to find him and train him without revealing the plan until the time is right.

The pastor should select a person who has a love for the culture and who is loyal to his dreams and leadership. He must be- or become- a qualified leader with sound character. A holy walk with God is indispensable. He must be submissive to the pastor and his principles.

The program must be mapped out. The goal should be to bring ethnic men and women into a living relationship with Jesus Christ. They need to be saved! The same principles apply to all people everywhere. Sin must be eradicated, and a holy life initiated.

A Sunday school class in the ethnic language can be of great value. The constituency can then invite their ethnic language speaking friends to attend. Bible classes in the homes of the ethnic constituents are great means of winning souls and may develop into a branch church.

Once the church has won a nucleus of a minority language speaking group to Christ, and has adopted them into the church family, the pastor can begin the process of developing that group into a church.

The pastor must be patient and wait for the precious fruit to mature. Ethnic constituents make wonderful members, and when properly developed, they will become dedicated witness to the community. Sacrifice is not new to them, and generosity is one of their virtues. They are also great soul winners.

The United Pentecostal Church International can reap a rich harvest of any culture by having a goal not just to house them, but to pour into them a burden to reach their own. We will lose some from our local churches as a result, but in many instances they will return to native countries. This need not be a negative, but when it takes place, let it become an extension of our churches. They will enrich us with the greatest treasure of all-lost souls withdrawn as brands plucked from the fire.

By God's grace we can stage a spiritual battle that will make history. Let us dream big dreams!

Mothers and fathers in our modern days are struggling in private to cope with the flood of changes that are being forced upon them. They see a past that leaves them as a wisp of smoke from a dying campfire. For this they fear the changes that are all but inevitable.

What I write is not to produce guilt in our generation, for we can neither correct the wrongs of the past, nor untangle the knotty cords of history. However, we can, as a church, understand the turmoil that fills the hearts of others we are endeavoring to reach with the gospel, and accept the fact that some of our forefathers were not without blame in many actions to establish the society we know.

Can we not repent before God for those things we recognize as wrong, and build upon those things that were right, until our world can know that there is a 'people' who radiate the love of Christ before the voice of the archangel declares the end of our activity?

Now let's step to the front and lead the battle into another dimension. Let's sit down and chart our path to some effective evangelism programs that will see great numbers among all cultures, both in the United States and Canada, and allow them an opportunity to drink from the fountains of life. Wouldn't it be great if we could just bury the old ugly past, and clasp a hand a bit darker than our own, and say, we love you! We are all the creation of the Almighty God. We are His children. I believe with this attitude we can reach our world with this saving message. Worth an attempt, don't you think!